THE PASSION OF
CHRIST
THROUGH THE
EYES OF MARY

THE PASSION OF CHRIST

THROUGH THE EYES OF MARY

SAINT ANSELM OF CANTERBURY
AND OTHERS

COMPILED AND TRANSLATED BY
FR. ROBERT NIXON, OSB

TAN Books
Gastonia, North Carolina

Translated by Fr. Robert Nixon, OSB

Cover design by Andrew Schmalen

Cover image credit: Pieta, 1876 (oil on canvas), Bouguereau, William-Adolphe (1825-1905), © Christie's Images / Bridgeman Images.

ISBN: 978-1-5051-2797-3
Kindle ISBN: 978-1-5051-2798-0
ePUB ISBN: 978-1-5051-2799-7

Published in the United States by

TAN Books
PO Box 269
Gastonia, NC 28053
www.TANBooks.com

Printed in the United States of America

By the cross her station keeping,
Stood the mournful Mother weeping,
Close to Jesus till the last:
Through her heart, His sorrow sharing,
All His bitter torments bearing,
Now at length the sword has passed.
Mother! Holy font of love!
Touch my spirit from above,
Make my heart with thine accord:
Make me feel as thou hast felt;
Make my soul to burn and melt
With the love of Christ my Lord.

From *Stabat Mater Dolorosa*,
attributed to Jacapone da Todi

CONTENTS

The Book of the Passion of Our Lord

Our Lady's Lament

The Rosary of the Seven Sorrows of Mary

TRANSLATOR'S NOTE

PRAYERFUL MEDITATION ON the blessed passion of Christ is a wonderfully inspiring and venerable devotional practice, one of the greatest treasures of our Catholic spirituality. In a sense, it is as ancient as Christianity itself, since the Gospels each portray the passion of Christ in vivid and moving ways. But in the High Middle Ages, from about the eleventh century onwards, there was a renewed and intense focus on the sufferings and death of Christ. This renewed focus on the human sufferings of Christ was both reflected in and developed by the passionate writings of saints like Anselm of Canterbury and Bernard of Clairvaux. The Blessed Virgin Mary was, of course, central to this highly incarnational spirituality. It was she who stood faithfully by the cross, and it was she who, more than any other, shared the pains of her beloved Son and felt them as if they were her very own.

This volume presents English translations of three extremely significant medieval works, meditating on the passion of Christ through the eyes of His glorious Mother. The first is the *Dialogue of the Blessed Virgin Mary and St. Anselm on the Passion of Our Lord*. This remarkable piece of devotional literature presents a touching colloquy between the Mother of God and Saint Anselm (1033–1109) in which the passion and death of Christ is described with great beauty and poignancy. This work is best appreciated as an example of "devotional creative writing" in which the author uses his imagination to paint a vivid image of the events surrounding Our Lord's death. Naturally, a synthesis of the narratives of the various Gospel accounts are the basis of the dialogue, but other striking details are added as well to provide a more complete picture. Of course, whether these additional details are understood as elements of private revelation or simply devotional imagination, they should not be interpreted as making any claims to objective historicity. Rather, they serve to assist in prayer and meditation on these most awesome and heartrending events.

The second work is entitled the *Liber de Passione Christi* (*Book of the Passion of Christ*). Like Saint Anselm's dialogue, it is also presented in the form of a colloquy with Mary on the passion of Jesus, but the interlocutor in this instance is Saint Bernard of Clairvaux (1090–1153). Indeed, the work is traditionally attributed to that great saint. For various philological and stylistic reasons, this attribution seems unlikely, although it is by no means impossible. Regardless of the authorship, the work was an extremely popular and widely circulated devotional text throughout the second half of the Middle Ages, and many manuscript copies of it survive.

The third text is *Our Lady's Lament*. Unlike the other works included here, this tract was originally composed in Middle English. While the author cannot be determined with certainty, it is considered most likely to have been written by John Lydgate (1370–1451), an English Benedictine monk and poet. The version of it offered here translates the text into comprehensible Modern English, but a few easily understood verbal anachronisms have been deliberately retained for the sake of emulating the tone and character of the original.

Finally, the traditional method of praying the *Rosary of the Seven Sorrows of Mary* is also included in the form of a translation of the booklet entitled *Corona dolorosa, seu modus pie meditandi dolores praecipuos B. V. Mariae*,[1] published in 1738. This wonderful and highly efficacious method of praying the Rosary, which is especially associated with the Servite Order, involves meditation upon each of the traditional seven sorrows of Our Lady. It consists of the

---

[1] *The Sorrowful Crown, or a Method of Piously Meditating on the Principal Sorrows of the Blessed Virgin Mary.*

Hail Mary prayed in seven groups of seven, with the Lord's Prayer at the beginning of each group. Short aspirations or intentions are attached to each prayer. This most beautiful and touching form of the Marian Rosary has been officially approved by the Holy See, with Popes Benedict XIII, Clement XII, and Leo XIII each extending particular indulgences to those who pray it. Details of these are also included in the introductory notes to this Rosary.

The works collected here each offer profound and moving perspectives into the sufferings and death of Christ through the eyes of Mary. These sufferings should always be close to the heart of every Christian, as they are the highest and most noble expression of God's infinite love and mercy. In looking at Jesus through the eyes of His glorious Mother, we are looking at our Savior from the perspective of the one who was closer to Him than any other, who shared His pains and joys more intimately than any other, and who loved Him more passionately, more totally, and more faithfully than any other. Let us each strive to love Jesus in that manner, to gaze upon Him through the eyes of Mary, and to love Him with her most Immaculate Heart. *Ad Jesum per Mariam!*

Fr. Robert Nixon, OSB
Abbey of the Most Holy Trinity
New Norcia, Western Australia

DIALOGUE OF THE BLESSED VIRGIN MARY AND SAINT ANSELM ON THE PASSION OF OUR LORD

INTRODUCTION

SAINT ANSELM HAD for a long time prayed earnestly to the glorious Virgin Mary that she would reveal to him the mysteries of her divine Son's suffering and death. His prayers were accompanied with ardent weeping and prolonged fasting.

At last, the Blessed Virgin appeared before the saint. She spoke to him the following words, "My beloved Son suffered such terrible things that no one could possibly describe them without a profuse outpouring of tears! Nevertheless, because I have now been glorified with all the glory of heaven and rejoice in the Lord's resurrection, I am no longer able to weep; all my former pain and bitter sorrow has been transformed into exultant and inexpressible joy! Therefore I myself shall speak to you of my Son's passion, narrating its events in due order."

Saint Anselm therefore proceeded to address questions to Mary, and she answered each one in turn. [The dialogue which ensued is recorded in the following pages.]

1

THE BETRAYAL OF CHRIST AND HIS PRAYER IN THE GARDEN OF GETHSEMANE

Anselm: TELL ME, MOST beloved Lady, how did the events of the passion of your Son first begin?

Mary: When my Son and His disciples had arisen from the table at His last supper, the perfidious traitor Judas Iscariot went forth alone to see the high priests of the temple. He received from them the sum of thirty denarii of silver and, in exchange, promised to betray Christ into their hands.

Anselm: What type of denarii was it which he received from the priests?

Mary: They were the denarii of the Ishmaelites. In fact, they were the very same coins which the brothers of Joseph had received from the Ishmaelites when they sold him into slavery[1] some two thousand years previously.[2] Through succession and inheritance, these same thirty silver denarii had passed into the hands of the temple treasury. Each of these silver coins was ten times the size and weight of a usual denarius.[3] Judas was so avaricious and filled with such a greed for earthly wealth that when he saw these coins, he immediately undertook to betray my Son to the temple priests. Indeed, Christ had foreseen this act of betrayal and had often spoken of it, but even this did not serve to deter Judas from his wicked purpose.

Anselm: My Lady, were you present at that last supper with your Son and His disciples?

Mary: No, I was not present when my Son partook of that last supper at which He washed the feet of His disciples and spoke to them loving words of encouragement. This was the great and holy supper in which He gave to them

---

[1] The source of this curious detail is not clear. It perhaps reflects legends in circulation at the time.

[2] The Latin text has "4,000 years" here, but this is almost certainly a simple scribal error. Traditional datings based on Scripture place the selling of Joseph into slavery as occurring about 2,000 years before the time of Christ.

[3] The Latin text reads that each of the denarii "*valuit decem usuales*" (i.e., that each coin was of ten times the value of a usual coin). Yet since the value of coins in those days depended upon the actual amount of metal from which they were formed, the translation has been adjusted to reflect this. The source of this detail may again have been legends in circulation at the time.

His own Body and Blood through the sacramental signs of bread and wine. After this sacred meal, when Judas went to see the high priests to betray Jesus, Christ went on with His disciples to Mount Sion, passing through the gate by the Pool of Siloam. My Son then entered a garden. And while the disciples slept, He went forth to the foot of the Mount of Olives so that He was about a stone's throw from the sleeping disciples. And there, He poured out fervent prayers to His heavenly Father, saying:

> "O Lord, hear my cry!
> For thou art kind and full of compassion.
> According to the abundance of thy mercy, look upon me now.
> Turn not thy face from thy Child!
> I am gravely afflicted; give ear to my supplications.
> Look upon my soul, and free it from the tribulation and peril which surrounds it.
> Rescue me, I implore thee, from the snares of my enemies;
> Save me from the clutches of all those who seek to destroy my life!"[4]

Anselm: Most glorious Virgin, why was it that your Son—who was both Son of God and true God Himself—needed to pray at that time?

---

[4] See Psalm 67:17–19.

Mary: Although He knew Himself to be the Son of God, still He needed to pray for three reasons: Firstly, He was of a delicate and refined constitution, as the child of an inviolate virgin, and born of royal blood. For it is a fact that those who are more noble suffer more deeply when they are harmed than those who are of coarse and common stock. Secondly, He experienced such an extremity of anguish that His sweat ran forth like great drops of blood. [Thirdly,] because, being God Himself, He knew perfectly in advance everything which He was to suffer and undergo. This included the contemptuous showering of Him with spittle, the blasphemies and insults of the soldiers and the crowds, the bloody scourging, the cruel crucifixion, and all the innumerable other torments He was to endure.

For a common thief may know that he has been sentenced to death, but he does not fully know in advance the exact nature of the pains of death which he shall experience until he is actually hanging from the noose by his neck. But my Son, being true God as well as true Man, knew what the future held so perfectly that He felt everything in advance. Accordingly, He prayed, "Father, if it is possible, let this chalice pass me by! But let not my will, but Thine, be done."[5] And when He had uttered this prayer, an angel appeared before Him and imbued Him with strength and courage, saying, "Be brave, my Lord, for now you are about to redeem the entire human race!"

---

[5] Matthew 26:39.

2

THE ARREST OF CHRIST

[Mary continues her reply to Anselm.]

AFTER THIS, MY Son returned to His disciples and found that they had succumbed to sleep. He said to them with some disappointment, "Could you not remain awake for just one hour with Me?"[6] And He added, "Behold! The one who will betray Me now draws nigh."[7] Just at that time, Judas appeared on the scene, together with a large crowd of the temple priests and guards. Now there were two amongst those in the garden who were of very similar appearance—namely, James and Jesus.[8] For this reason, [that is, in order

---

[6] Matthew 26:40.

[7] Mark 13:42.

[8] According to certain traditions, the apostle James (the cousin of Jesus, sometimes spoken of as "the brother of the Lord") was of very similar physical appearance to Jesus. The author proposes that this

to identify Jesus,] Judas said to the guards, "The one that I shall kiss—He is the man. Arrest Him."[9]

And when Judas approached, accompanied by the crowds, Jesus stepped forward and said, "Whom do you seek?" To this they responded, "Jesus the Nazarene." And Jesus answered them, "I am He!" And when He had replied thus, all of them fell to the ground overcome by a mysterious awe. My Son then repeated, "I am He." In this way, the words of Scripture were fulfilled, which declares, "Not one of those whom you have given me shall I lose."[10]

Then Judas approached Him and kissed Him. And Jesus said to him, "Judas, do you betray the Son of Man with a kiss?"[11] And then the guards and the officers seized Him and held Him.

At this point, Peter drew his sword and struck the servant of the high priest. The servant's name was Malchus.[12]

Anselm: Was there not a miracle which occurred at that time?

Mary: Yes, indeed! For my Son turned His attention to that injured servant and cured his wounded ear. And He said to Peter, "Return your sword to its sheath! For he who

---

resemblance was the reason that it is necessary for Judas to kiss Jesus in order to identify Him for the guards.

[9] Matthew 26:48.
[10] See John 18:4–9.
[11] Luke 12:48.
[12] See John 18:10.

lives by the sword shall die by the sword. Or do you think that I am not able to ask My Father in Heaven, Who would immediately send more than twelve legions of angels to defend Me?"[13] At this point, all the disciples took to flight, leaving my Son alone in the power of His enemies.

Anselm: Tell me, my Lady, were you also there when these things happened?

Mary: No, I was not.

Anselm: Why was that, since you love Him so dearly?

Mary: Night had then fallen, and it was not proper for a young woman (such as I then was) to be outdoors at that time.

Anselm: Most sweet Lady, where were you then when these things transpired?

Mary: I was in the house of my sister, the mother of the apostles James and John.

Anselm: How and by whom were you informed of what had happened to your Son in the garden?

Mary: Hear me, O Anselm, for what I have to tell you is truly lamentable! The disciples came running to me, their eyes filled with tears. They cried out to me, "O most dear Mistress, your beloved Son and our Master has been captured! They have taken Him away, bound, and we do not know where, nor what has become of Him, nor even if He is alive or dead."

---

13 Matthew 26:32–33.

Anselm: My Lady, you must surely then have wept yourself?

Mary: Indeed. For though I knew full well that my Son was to redeem the human race through His death and glorious resurrection, at that moment because of my maternal affection the sword of which Simeon had spoken prophetically passed through my very heart![14]

---

[14] See Luke 2:35.

3

CHRIST IS LED BEFORE ANANIAS, AND PETER DENIES HIM THREE TIMES

Anselm: WHERE, O MARY, did they lead your beloved Son then?

Mary: From the garden of Gethsemane, they led Him through the Valley of Josaphat and through the Golden Gate of the city. Then He was led into the palace of the scribes and Pharisees—that is, to the house of Ananias. Ananias began to question Him about His teaching and His disciples. To this, my Son responded, "I have always spoken openly when I was in the world, and I have taught publicly in the synagogues and in the temples where all the Jews come together. There is nothing which I have said in secret. Why, therefore, do you question Me about My teaching?

Ask any of those who have heard Me about what I have taught, for these all know and can tell it to you."[15]

Then, with callous cruelty, one of the officers present slapped Him on His dear face, saying, "Is that any way to answer a high priest?" But my Son, the tender Lamb of God, answered him, "If there is anything wrong or improper in what I have said, point it out to Me. But if I have spoken the truth, why, then, do you slap Me?"[16]

Then they blindfolded His eyes as if He were a common thief. This act of degradation is something normally done to no one, unless they have already been judged and found guilty! And, for the whole night, they did not cease from mocking and humiliating Him, spitting in His face and striking Him. They said to Him with scornful derision, "Prophesy to us, O Prophet! Who is it that is striking you?"[17]

At this time, the apostle John was within the palace, for he was known to the high priest. He led Peter in with him. A certain maidservant saw Peter and recognized him, saying, "You are surely one of His disciples, aren't you?" But Peter, with an oath, repeatedly denied having known Him, nor even ever to have seen Him. And, after he had denied Him thus three times, immediately a cock crowed. At that moment, Jesus turned and gazed at Peter. Peter recalled

---

[15] John 18:20.
[16] John 18:22–23.
[17] Matthew 26:28.

the words of the Lord, when He had said, "Before the cock crows, you will have denied Me three times!" And Peter went out and wept bitterly.

Anselm: Where were you, most dear Lady, when these things were taking place?

Mary: As soon as the disciples had told me about the arrest of my Son, it was as if all my bones had melted within me from grief and terror! Nevertheless, I arose and, together with Mary Magdalene, went forth to the temple and the palace of the high priest. There we heard the tumult which was taking place in the house of Ananias. We wished to enter, but were not permitted to do so.

So I stood outside, lamenting and crying. "Alas!" I exclaimed. "O my beloved Son, You are the very light of my eyes! Who shall give oceans of tears to my eyes so that I may weep enough for this misery which awaits You?" [For I knew in my heart that His passion was drawing near.]

Mary Magdalene, meanwhile, was wandering to-and-fro restlessly, seeking to see or hear what was taking place and striving to gain some knowledge of what was happening inside through a window. Perchance, she happened to hear Peter's denials of Christ. How great was the sorrow and anxiety which pierced her heart when she heard those dreadful words whereby the man who had been chosen as the leader of the disciples abandoned his beloved Master! She cried out in tones of poignant desolation and love, "O my dear Jesus, what shall become of You when even Your most trusted follower and the leader of Your disciples has thus denied You? O sweet Jesus, *I* shall never deny You, though I live for all eternity."

I myself stood there as if paralyzed with grief. Everything which my Son suffered—the blows and mockery and the pain of Peter's denial of Him—I felt myself as if they were happening to me. After Peter had denied the Lord three times, he came out from the priestly palace. He saw Mary Magdalene and myself standing there, both weeping. Touched with sorrow, I said to him, "O Peter, tell me, what has become of Jesus, and where is my precious Son now?" He cried out in a voice filled with tears and said, "Alas, most dear Lady, they have handled Him without mercy, and I fear that they shall torture Him to death!" And rushing forth from there terrified, he hid himself amongst the clefts of the great boulder known as Gallicantus.[18] And he was not seen again until after Jesus had died upon the cross.

Anselm: Tell me, noble Lady, how did you react when you heard Peter tell you about what had happened to Jesus?

Mary: At that moment, the sword of sorrow, of which Simeon had prophesied, was again driven into my poor heart!

---

[18] Literally, "He hid himself in the stone which was called 'Gallicantus.'" *Gallicantus* means "the crow of a rooster." There is an ancient church known as the Basilica of St. Peter *in Gallicantu* on the slopes of Mount Zion, just outside the walls of the old city of Jerusalem, which appears to be attached to this tradition.

4

CHRIST IS LED TO CAIAPHAS

Anselm: PLEASE TELL ME, beloved Mother of God, what happened after this?

Mary: In the morning, He was led from the house of Ananias to Caiaphas, who was the supreme high priest at that time. As He was taken forth, it was then that I saw Him for the first time since He had been captured. How I rushed to Him, like an anxious lioness which has been separated from her precious cub! As I saw His tender face besmeared with spittle, I gave voice to my maternal anguish, crying out through my tears: "O my Child! How miserable now does Your holy face appear, the face whose beauty and sweetness have given me such indescribable joy!"

Of course, I longed to embrace Him in my arms, but the guards would not permit me to do so. Instead, they pushed me back and forth roughly, deriding and insulting me. And a mob of onlookers gathered to jeer, as if some common thief or bandit had been captured and deservedly condemned.

Anselm: But did you have any hope that He might be liberated from His plight?

Mary: Indeed I did. For I knew that He was eloquent in speech and extremely intelligent. I therefore certainly hoped that He could defend Himself convincingly against any judge. But when He came before His judge, He stood like a gentle lamb before His slaughterer, not opening His mouth! Truly, I also hoped that the very beauty and honesty of His face would suffice to stir up pity and trust in the heart of anyone who judged Him. Yet by the time He reached His trial, He had been slapped and spat upon to such an extent that the comeliness of His countenance had come to be concealed, and His nobility was no longer to be seen. What was more, many false witnesses rose up against Him, declaring Him to be a destroyer of the law, a troublemaker who was arousing the people to sedition. At last, two such false witnesses spoke against Him, saying, "He declared that He was able to destroy the temple of God, and in three days to rebuild it."[19]

---

[19] Matthew 26:60–61.

Caiaphas demanded of Him, "Tell us if You are the Christ." To this interrogation, He replied, "If I tell you, you will not believe Me. And if I question you, you shall not answer Me.[20] But I tell you solemnly, you will see the Son of Man seated at the right hand of the glory of God, and coming upon the clouds of heaven!" Then the chief priest tore his vestments and exclaimed, "What need have we of further witnesses? You have all heard His blasphemy from His own mouth! What do you think should be done?" And all of those assembled cried out, "He is deserving of death!"[21]

As this fateful and dreaded sentence was pronounced by the priestly assembly, the cruel and bitter sword of which Simeon had spoken was once more thrust into my heart!

---

[20] Luke 22:67–68.
[21] Matthew 26:64–66.

5

CHRIST APPEARS
BEFORE PILATE

Anselm: WHERE, O MARY, was your Son taken after this had occurred?

Mary: He was taken before the Roman governor and judge, Pilate.

Anselm: At this time, was there anything for which you were hoping, dearest Lady?

Mary: I hoped for much then! For my Son had often spoken words of gentle sweetness and divine wisdom to the crowds. He had healed a great number of those afflicted with illnesses of all kind, and had fed the multitudes in the desert in a miraculous manner with a few loaves and fish. I believed that these multitudes, who owed Him such a debt of gratitude, must surely be eager to set Him free from

His captors. How appalled and disappointed I was when I heard them cry out with one voice in the presence of Pilate, "Crucify Him! Crucify Him!"[22] The crowds asserted that He had declared Himself to be the Son of God[23] and had refused to pay the taxes due to Caesar.[24]

Then Pilate questioned Him about the nature of His kingdom, asking Him, "Are You the King of the Jews?" To this Jesus replied, "Do you ask this of your own accord or have others spoken to you about Me?" Pilate answered, "Am I a Jew? Your own people and the chief priests of Your own religion have handed You over to me. Tell me, what is it that You have done?" But to this, Jesus responded, "My Kingdom is not of this world. If My Kingdom were of this world, My servants would have fought for Me and never have permitted Me to be arrested." Pilate was troubled by these words and asked Him, "You are a king, then?" To this Jesus answered, "It is you who say so. Yes, I am a King. For this purpose was I born, for this I came into the world: that I should give testimony to the Truth. And everyone who is of this Truth shall hear My voice." Pilate was perplexed and said, "Truth! What is that?"[25] Christ, my Son, chose not to answer this question. For He knew that if He

---

[22] Luke 23:21.
[23] Matthew 27:43.
[24] Luke 23:2.
[25] John 18:33–38.

did answer it, Pilate would have released Him, and then the human race would never have been redeemed.

Meanwhile, Judas Iscariot saw that my Son had been arrested and faced condemnation. He realized the unprecedented treachery of his act of betrayal and bitterly regretted his crime. So he took the thirty pieces of silver and hurried to the assembly of the high priests and elders of the people. He exclaimed, "I have sinned, for I have betrayed One Who is entirely just!" But they responded, "What do your scruples matter to us? But you shall see [the full meaning of your actions]!" And Judas hurled the silver to the ground before them and rushed out of the temple. He then went off to a deserted place and, overcome with shame and despair, hanged himself.[26]

At that time, Pilate called to himself an assembly of all the high priests, the magistrates, and the people. He announced to them, "Out of all your accusations, I can find no case against this man which would merit the sentence of death." But the crowd persisted in their demands for his execution, saying, "He has stirred up and agitated the people throughout all of Judea, beginning from Galilee and extending even to here!"[27]

---

[26] Matthew 27:3–5.
[27] Luke 23:4, 14.

6

JESUS IS BROUGHT BEFORE HEROD, THEN RETURNED TO PILATE

[Mary continues her reply to Anselm.]

ONCE PILATE HAD heard the crowd mention Galilee and had learned that Jesus was a Galilean, he resolved to send Him to Herod, [since Herod had juridical responsibility for that region]. Now, it happened that at that time Herod was present in Jerusalem.

When Herod set his eyes upon Jesus, he rejoiced greatly. For he had wished to see Him for some time, having heard much about Him. Indeed, he was eagerly hoping to witness some sign or miracle from Him. He questioned Jesus about a great many things. First of all, he asked Him if He had been the same infant Whom His father, [the earlier King Herod], had wished to kill, and on Whose account a multitude of innocent children had been slaughtered. Then he asked Him if He was the one Who had given sight to the man born blind, Who had raised up Lazarus from the tomb, Who had revived the deceased son of the widow at the gates of the city of Nain, and Who had performed innumerable other miracles besides these? Herod implored Him also to give him some display of His marvelous powers or to work some wonder in his sight, promising to rescue Him from the hands of His persecutors if He did so. But Jesus offered him no reply.

Herod even placed a crown upon His head, earnestly pledging to make Him a sharer of his royal power and equal co-heir to the throne if only He would perform a miracle for him.[28] Now, these crowns [of the type with which Herod placed on the head of Christ] are used by the Roman authorities to designate those whom they have recognized as local monarchs. But again, Jesus did not make any

---

[28] This coronation by Herod should not be confused with the crowning of Christ with thorns, which occurs later. There is, of course, no mention of the present incident in the canonical Gospels. It should therefore be read as part of a private revelation or imaginative reflection, and therefore need not be understood as necessarily possessing historical veracity. It does, however, seem to be consistent with the identification of Christ as the "King of the Jews," both by the crowds and the authorities.

answer. Meanwhile, the chief priests and the scribes stood by accusing Him.

Anselm: Most sweet Lady, did you still entertain any hopes for your Son's acquittal? And, if so, for what reason?

Mary: Yes, I still hoped! For I knew that Herod was imbued with a certain natural decency and dignity,[29] and therefore I hoped that he would spare my Son, Who was a man of manifest excellence and quality. But, alas, in the end he spurned my dear Son! Clothing Him in a garment of white, he had Him sent back to Pilate to deal with Him. And on that very day, Herod and Pilate, who had hitherto been enemies, became firm friends.[30]

Pilate knew full well the virulence of the cruelty and envy with which some of the temple authorities conspired to bring about the death of my Son. So he sent forth certain Roman guards to lead Him safely from Herod to himself, lest He be murdered along the way. Once Jesus had been returned to his custody, he called together all His accusers and said to them, "You have brought to me this man as if He is one stirring up sedition and rebellion amongst the people. But I have examined Him in your presence and cannot find any case against Him, out of all the many things of which

---

[29] In the Latin, the expression here is "*naturalis elegantiae*" (very literally, "of natural elegance"). The terms "decency and dignity" given in the present translation seem best to accord with the context.

[30] Luke 23:11–12.

you have accused Him. And neither did Herod, for he has returned Him to me. Truly, He is guilty of nothing which deserves death! I therefore propose to admonish Him and reprimand Him, and then to set Him free."[31]

But the gathered assembly all cried out that he should release to them Barabbas instead. This Barabbas had been imprisoned for sedition and murder. Pilate said a second time, "Why? What harm has He done? I can find no cause for sentencing Him to death. I shall reprimand Him and then release Him!"

But the crowd was insistent and demanded in a loud voice that He should be crucified. "Crucify Him! Crucify Him!" they shouted.[32] At that time, as Pilate was seated upon his judicial chair, his wife sent to him a message. "Do nothing to this innocent man!" was her plea. "For I have been greatly troubled in my dreams this night on account of Him."[33]

---

[31] Luke 23:14–16.
[32] Luke 23:21–22.
[33] Matthew 27:19.

7

THE SCOURGING AND THE CROWNING WITH THORNS

[Mary continues her reply to Anselm.]

PILATE [HIMSELF BECAME afraid and did not wish to put Christ to death.] Hoping to assuage the cruelty of His persecutors, he had Jesus bound to a pillar and scourged so that "from the soles of His feet to His head, there was no part of Him which escaped harm."[34] This pillar was of such a width that it was not possible for His two hands to reach when He stretched His arms around it. Hence the guards used a rope to bind His hands and hold Him in place.

Anselm: Beloved Lady, at that time did you still hope that He might escape the sentence of death?

---

[34] Isaiah 1:6.

Mary: I still hoped for much then! And I shall reveal to you, Anselm, my reasons for this. I knew that, in addition to His divine sanctity of soul, He possessed a visible nobility, gentleness, and beauty in His physical form. Once His outer garment was removed and Pilate and the assembly beheld His beauty and nobility of form, I firmly believed that they would be overcome with such a feeling of compassion that they would be moved to spare Him. But alas! By that time, His dear body was so covered in blood, gore, and wounds that His beauty and nobility were no longer visible.[35] On the contrary, He looked as if He was horribly deformed and stupefied, like one consumed by leprosy![36]

And the cruel soldiers, weaving a crown out of thorns, placed it upon His innocent head and robed Him with purple. They approached Him and said with bitter mockery, "Hail, King of the Jews!" And they slapped Him.[37]

This same crown of thorns is today in the possession of the king of France.[38] And it was not made from the common

---

[35] See Isaiah 53:2.

[36] See Isaiah 52:14.

[37] John 19:2–3.

[38] According to ancient tradition, the emperor Justinian presented the sacred relic of the original crown of thorns to St. Germain, the bishop of Paris, in the sixth century. Throughout most of the Middle Ages, this sacred object (which does indeed consist of rushes, as is described here) was in the possession of French kings. The same relic was preserved at Notre Dame Cathedral in Paris until 2019, when it was transferred to the Louvre Museum.

variety of thorn but of the type of rushes which grow by the sea. These rushes have sharper and more piercing spikes than common thorns. After beating Him with the rod of a spear, the soldiers pressed this crown so firmly into Him that blood gushed down His face! And thus gruesomely adorned, Pilate led Him before the people and said, "Behold, your King!" But the heartless mob cried out, "Take Him away! Take Him away and crucify Him!"[39]

In exasperation, Pilate answered them, "Take Him away yourselves and crucify Him!" But they replied, "We have a law, and according to that law He must die. For He has declared Himself to be the Son of God." When Pilate heard these words, he became even more fearful.

Anxiously, he reentered the praetorium and said to Jesus, "Who *are* You? And where do You come from?" But Jesus did not reply. Pilate said to Him, "Do You refuse to speak to me? Do You not know that I have the power to have You killed and also the power to set You free?" To this, Jesus replied, "You would have no power against Me were it not given to you from above. Therefore those who have handed Me over to you have the greater sin." Having heard this, Pilate anxiously sought for some way of releasing Him. But the Pharisees and scribes cried out, "If you release Him, then You are no friend of Caesar!"[40]

---

[39] John 19:14–15.
[40] John 19:6–12.

Pilate saw that his attempts to acquit Christ were in vain and that, on the contrary, the crowd was becoming more and more agitated and insistent. So he called for a dish of water to be brought to him and washed his hands in the view of all the people. He said, "I am innocent of the blood of this just man, as you can see." To this, all the people cried out, "Let His blood be upon us and upon our descendants!"[41] And they insisted with noisy tumult that He should be crucified. Alas, in the end, their voices prevailed. Pilate reluctantly consented to their demand. And he released the criminal [Barabbas], who had been incarcerated for homicide, in accordance with the request of the mob.[42]

---

[41] Matthew 27:24–25.
[42] Luke 28:23–25.

8

JESUS IS SENTENCED TO DEATH AND CARRIES HIS CROSS

[Mary continues her reply to Anselm.]

As IT WAS clear that the crowd could not be assuaged in any other way, Pilate then pronounced the sentence of death against my Son. He said, "I hereby sentence Jesus the Nazarene to death and order that He shall be executed by crucifixion."

Anselm: Most noble Lady, how did you react when you heard this dreaded sentence being pronounced against your dear Son?

Mary: When I heard these grim and fateful words, the piercing sword of which Simeon had spoken again passed through my heart!

Anselm: O sweet and cherished Mary! What happened after this?

Mary: They then took Jesus, my beloved Son, and led Him forth—as the apostle and evangelist John has written—carrying His cross. And they went to the place known as Calvary, where He was to be crucified.[43]

The cross was of such a great size that its total length was some fifteen feet. Now, my Son was thoroughly exhausted after all He had endured on the previous day and night, to such an extent that He was unable to sustain the heavy weight of His cross. Hence it was—as the evangelist Luke writes in his Gospel—that they took a certain Simon of Cyrene and placed the cross upon him to carry after Jesus, my precious and only-begotten Son.[44] But they did this not because they felt any compassion or kindness but rather because Jesus Himself was utterly unable to sustain the burden by Himself.

Anselm: As He was led forth with the cross, were there any who followed Him along the way?

Mary: There were. In fact, a whole crowd followed Him, just as happens when thieves and bandits are taken forth to be executed. Hence it is that Saint Luke writes, "A great multitude of the people followed Him. And amongst these

---

[43] John 19:16–18.
[44] Luke 23:26.

were many women, who mourned and lamented for Him."[45] But there followed Him also many wicked and malicious boys, who threw stones at Him.

My Son, Jesus, turned to the women who grieved for Him and said to them, "Daughters of Jerusalem, weep not for Me but for yourself and for your children—these ones who are now throwing stones and mud at Me! Truly, they know not what they do. For soon the day will come when they shall say that those who are childless are fortunate. They shall say that the womb that has never carried and infant is lucky, and that the breasts which have never nursed a baby are blessed! And they shall say to the mountains, 'Fall upon us!' and to the hills, 'Cover us!' For if your children commit these acts of cruelty now while the wood is still green—that is, while they are but children—what crimes and horrors shall they commit by the time the wood has become dry—that is, once they are mature?[46] And if they inflict such sufferings and ignominy on Me, what atrocities and cruelties shall future generations not do to the saints who follow Me?"

And they led with Him two other men who were also condemned to be crucified. This was done for the purpose of generating greater confusion and tumult amongst the crowds.

---

[45] Luke 23:27.
[46] Luke 23:28, 31.

9

THE SORROWFUL MEETING[47] OF CHRIST AND HIS MOTHER

[Mary continues her reply to Anselm.]

THUS THEY LED my Son as the principal condemned man amongst the group, and the two thieves as companions to Him. They went beyond the city gates, all the while hounded by the crowds of people pressing in upon them and hurling scorn and insults at them.

---

[47] Interestingly, the Greek word for "meeting" is used here, "*hypapante*." This is also the word used to designate the feast of the Presentation of Our Lord, and it seems probable that the author was wishing to suggest a certain parallel between these two events by his unusual choice of word.

I myself desperately wished to follow Him closely, but—alas!—I could not, because of the sheer density of the crowd. But nevertheless, I deliberated with Mary Magdalene, who was my companion at that time. Together, we took an alternative route, passing through a certain field and going around a spring of water until we met with them all on the way.

When I finally saw Him again, my Son was in a wretched condition and looked like one weighed down with pain and anguish. But as He passed by, He gently inclined Himself to me and said, "I thank you, My beloved and chosen Mother, for the countless benefits which you have bestowed upon Me and for the trials, tribulations, and deprivations which you have endured for My sake! For it was you who nourished the temple of My mortal body with maternal care. And now, in My hour of pain and disgrace, you have not abandoned Me. Nor have you permitted yourself to be overcome with shame or fear, although I am now reduced to being an object of scorn and contempt and despised by all."

10

THE CRUCIFIXION AND RAISING UP OF THE CROSS

[Mary continues her reply to Anselm.]

AFTER THEY HAD arrived at that place called Calvary, there they crucified Him, and the two thieves with Him, one on His right and the other on His left.[48]

Anselm: How did they do this?

Mary: Hear, Anselm, and I shall tell you. What I have to relate is profoundly lamentable and of infinite bitterness. And none of the Evangelists have recorded these dreadful things in the sacred pages of their holy books.

They came to the hill called Calvary, a wretched and deplorable place, where carcasses of dogs and the corpses of beggars and lepers are discarded. And they stripped my dear

---

[48] Mark 15:27.

Son of all His clothing, leaving Him completely exposed. I myself, as I looked on, felt barely alive, so weakened was I with horror and shock. Nevertheless, I took the veil which I wore on my head and wrapped it around His waist to provide Him with some covering [for the sake of modesty].

Then the soldiers placed His cross upon the ground and stretched Him upon it. They hammered the first nail [into one of His hands]. It was of such great width that, at that time, no blood could gush forth. For the nail filled the wound entirely and firmly. After this, they took a rope and bound His other arm to the wood of the cross and hammered in the second nail in the same way. Following this, both of His feet were tied to the cross. They affixed these with a single nail of the most cruel and piercing sharpness.

His body was stretched so tightly on the cross that even His bones were visible. In this way, the words of the psalm were fulfilled, which say, "They could count every one of my bones."[49] And then was fulfilled another prophecy of David—or rather of Christ Himself—speaking through the psalm, in which it is written "Hear, my daughter, and see!"[50] This was as if my Son was saying, "Hear, My beloved Mother, the harsh sound of the hammers, and see how they cruelly affix My hands and feet to the wood of the cross! Truly, there is none to console Me or to have compassion for

---

[49] Psalm 21:18.
[50] Psalm 44:11.

Me, except you alone, My Mother. Hear Me, My daughter, and have pity on Me!" As I heard these words, the prophecy of fateful Simeon was again fulfilled, and the sword of anguish and pain was driven through my heart.

After this, they raised up the cross. This took a great deal of effort. It was of such a height that I was not able to touch His feet. And once He was raised up, because of the weight of His suspended body, all of His wounds burst open. Blood flowed forth in copious torrents from His hands and His feet.

At the time, I was wearing a kind of white sheet, as was the custom for religious women, which covered my head and my entire body. And, as I stood at the foot of the cross, this pure white garment became saturated with the streams of crimson blood which gushed from His precious body!

11

THE INSULTS WHICH CHRIST SUFFERED ON THE CROSS

Anselm: WHAT HAPPENED AFTER that, O holy Mary?

Mary: After they had so cruelly crucified my beloved Son, they divided His clothing amongst them. Since His undergarment was of a single, unsewn piece, they cast lots to determine which of them should take that. In this way, the oracle of the prophet was fulfilled, "They divided my vestments amongst themselves, and cast lots for my garment."[51]

And Pilate had an inscription placed above His head, in Hebrew, Greek, and Latin characters, which read, "Jesus Christ, the King of the Jews." But when the Pharisees read

---

[51] Matthew 27:36.

this, they told Pilate that he should not write, "King of the Jews," but, "This man claimed to be the King of the Jews." But Pilate answered them, "What I have written, I have written!"[52]

And those who passed by blasphemed Him. They shook their heads and said, "Ah! You would destroy the temple and rebuild it in three days. Well, save yourself! If you really are the Son of God, come down from this cross." The scribes and chief priests similarly mocked Him, saying, "He saved others, but He is not able to save Himself. If He is the King of Israel, let Him descend now from the cross. Then we shall believe in Him! He placed His trust in God—let God liberate Him now if He so wishes. For this man claimed to be the very Son of God!"[53]

---

[52] John 19:19–22.
[53] Matthew 27:39–43.

12

THE WORDS OF CHRIST FROM THE CROSS

Anselm: O MOTHER OF God, how did your divine Son respond to this heartless derision?

Mary: My beloved Child prayed for them. He implored God, "Father, forgive them, for they know not what they do."[54] But the crowds stood around, waiting to see what would happen next. And they, too, insulted Him.

It was then as if He spoke to me in my heart, saying, "Hear, My daughter, and see![55] Hear the voices of those who are so viciously mocking your Son, and see the grim anguish which I now undergo. You well know that it was by God's Holy Spirit that you conceived Me and that it was as a virgin

---

[54] Luke 23:34.
[55] Psalm 44:11.

that you bore Me into this world. You remember also how you nursed Me with tender care and love when I was but a small infant in your arms. Although all of this crowd refuses to believe in Me, I know that *you* have always believed in Me and that you now share with Me fully in all the agony of My sufferings." And as these words resounded in my heart, it was as if the sword of sorrow which Simeon foretold again passed through my soul.

When the thief, who had been crucified at His left side, heard the mockery of the crowd, he also insulted Him. He said, "If you are the Christ, save Yourself and us also!" But the other thief, who was at the right side of Jesus, reproofed him, saying, "Do you have no fear of God? For we are all receiving the same punishment, but we both have deserved it. But this man has committed no crime." And he said to Jesus, "Remember me, Lord, when You come into Your kingdom." And Jesus said to him, "I tell you solemnly, this day you shall be with Me in Paradise."[56]

Anselm: What did you do next, my Lady?

Mary: I stood by the cross, with my heart filled with such abject sorrow that I sought no consolation. And with me stood my sisters and Mary Magdalene.

---

[56] Luke 23:39–45.

And when my Son saw me and John, the disciple whom He loved, He said to me, "Woman, behold, your son." Then He said to the disciple, "Behold, your mother."[57]

This was around the sixth hour of the day.[58] And at that time heavy darkness fell upon the whole earth, until around the ninth hour.[59] And then Jesus cried out in a loud voice full of anguish, *"Eli, Eli lamma sabbacthani?"* That is, "My God, my God, why have You abandoned Me?" Upon hearing this, some of crowd called out, "Look, He is crying out! Let us see if Elisha comes to set Him free."[60]

When Jesus realized that all had been accomplished, He said, "I thirst!" For what, O Lord, did You thirst? You thirsted, indeed, for nothing but the salvation of sinners! But there was a vessel filled with vinegar nearby. One of the crowd rushed forth and filled a sponge with this vinegar and, placing it upon a spear, raised it to His mouth for Him to drink. He did this [not out of compassion] but only so that He would hasten on His death. And when He had tasted it, He said, "It is consummated."

---

[57] John 19:25–27.
[58] That is, around 12:00 noon.
[59] That is, around 3:00 p.m.
[60] Matthew 27:43–49.

13

THE DEATH OF CHRIST AND THE MIRACULOUS SIGNS WHICH FOLLOWED

[Mary continues her reply to Anselm.]

AFTER THIS, MY Son prayed aloud, "Father, into Your hands I commend My spirit."[61] This sincere and earnest prayer was accompanied by a great outflow of blood.

In this commendation of His spirit to God His Father, Christ commended also myself, His Mother. For I had served as the pure tabernacle of the spirit of which He spoke—that is, the Holy Spirit. And this commendation of myself to God the Father embraced also all the other souls who love and fear His name. For all holy souls become

---

[61] Luke 23:46.

dwelling places of the same Holy Spirit. And, altogether, we shall be victorious at the end of time![62]

After this, He bowed His head and gave up His spirit.[63] Then the veil of the temple was torn in two, from the top to the bottom. The earth shook, and the stones were torn apart. This was particularly the case with the large boulder upon which the cross itself stood. It was rent apart in such a way as to leave an opening large enough to insert a hand into. Tombs also opened up, and many of the bodies of the saints who rested within rose from the dead. Following the resurrection of my Son, many of these saints went out from their tombs and entered the holy city, where they were seen by many.

The centurion and those soldiers who were with Him, keeping watch over Jesus, witnessed the earthquakes and feared very greatly.[64] The centurion himself glorified God. He declared, "Truly, this man was the Son of God!"[65]

---

[62] The text in this paragraph refers to Mary in the third person, so it is not entirely clear whether it is intended to be a continuation of her discourse or an interjected commentary. In the present translation, it has been treated as part of her own discourse. However, to do this in a clear and idiomatic way, some minor modifications have been made—specifically using first-person pronouns for Mary and omitting certain expression of praise and devotion which it would seem incongruous for the Blessed Virgin to apply to herself.

[63] John 19:30.

[64] Matthew 27:51–54.

[65] Luke 23:47.

Behold! All things of the heavens and the earth were touched with deep compassion at the sufferings and death of Christ, even the inanimate and insensate elements of stone and earth! It was only those who persecuted Him who remained unmoved and whose hearts remained unsoftened.

Indeed, all who were present and had witnessed what had taken place struck their chests in grief and anguish. And all His relatives and friends stood some distance off, together with the women who had followed Him from Jerusalem and looked on at the dreadful events which had transpired.

14

THE LAMENTATION OF THE MOTHER FOR HER SON

Anselm: Most beloved Lady, had your sorrows reached their end at this point?

Mary: Alas no, Anselm! For the prophecy spoken by Simeon, that a sword would pass through my heart,[66] had not yet been fully consummated. You shall hear now of that which is lamentable above all else.

Being a day of preparation [for the Sabbath], the crowds requested that the bodies not remain on the cross for the Sabbath day itself, for it was a Sabbath of particular importance. They therefore asked Pilate that he should have the legs of the crucified men broken and their bodies removed. So the soldiers came and broke the legs of the two

---
[66] Luke 2:35.

thieves who had been crucified with Him. But when they came to Jesus Himself, they found that He was already dead. So they did not break His legs. Instead, one of the soldiers pierced His side with a lance, and immediately flowed forth blood mixed with water.

Upon witnessing this horrendous act of cruelty, which inflicted injury upon the body of one Who was already dead, I became like one who is almost dead myself! Only then was the fateful prophecy uttered by Simeon fully completed, in which he declared that a sword would pass through my heart.[67]

And then I broke down and began to cry and wail uncontrollably. But my tears now failed me, for I had cried with such profusion on the proceeding night and on that day already that my eyes were reduced to dryness. I exclaimed, "Oh, my beloved Son! Where now is the sweet consolation which I have always found in You? If only I could die with You now, my Jesus!"

And with these and similar outpourings of grief, I mourned the death of my cherished and only-begotten Child.

---

[67] This "sword of sorrow" has been described as passing through the Blessed Virgin heart now on a total of seven occasions, reflecting the tradition of the Seven Sorrows of Mary.

THE DESCENT OF THE SOUL OF CHRIST INTO LIMBO

[Mary continues her reply to Anselm.]

BUT, [DESPITE MY continuing lamentations], at that time there was great rejoicing in limbo. For the soul of Christ then descended into that shadowy realm armed with all His divine and radiant might. There, He liberated all the holy and God-fearing people of the past from their confinement. Indeed, He utterly destroyed limbo![68]

---

[68] The concept of *limbo* here is a place where the souls of righteous people who lived before the time of Christ would go, since (before the time of His death and resurrection) it was impossible for them to be admitted to heaven.

Moreover, He obstructed the very gates of hell in such a way that no Christian shall ever be compelled to enter into that fearsome place of torment unless they do so as a result of their own free will. He also made it so that no soul who has merited a sentence of damnation can ever leave until it faces the day of its Final Judgment.

16

CHRIST'S BODY IS REMOVED FROM THE CROSS AND PLACED IN THE TOMB

Anselm: MARY, WHAT HAPPENED after this?

Mary: After this, Joseph of Arimathea asked Pilate if he could take the body of Jesus.[69] He said to him, amongst other things, "Your Excellency, unless you take away this body quickly, the good woman who is the mother of this youth shall die from sheer sorrow!" Pilate inquired if He was already dead and learned from the centurion all that had occurred. And so he ordered the body of Jesus to be taken down. And the body was entrusted to Joseph, who took it away.

---

[69] John 19:38.

Anselm, hear something which is most lamentable and most grievously bitter! As the body of Jesus was taken down, I stood by the cross gazing upwards in desolation. As I saw His limbs being freed, I awaited eagerly to take His body in my arms and to kiss Him. And this I did. They placed His tender and wounded body upon the earth, about three feet from the cross. I held His head in my arms and began to weep tears of indescribable pain and bitterness. And I lamented thus, "Alas, my cherished Son! What consolation can I possibly have, now that I see my only Son dead before me?"

Then the evangelist John approached. He fell upon the chest of Jesus, mourning and crying out, "Oh! From this chest but yesterday I drank the sweetness of His holy words, but today, I draw from it only bitterness and pain!" Then Peter also approached. He recalled his three-fold denial of Christ and began also to weep in anguish. Then Mary Magdalene came. From her eyes flowed streams of tears, more profuse and unrelenting than all the others. She said, "Who shall forgive me my sins now that my beloved Lord has departed? Who shall defend me now from the condemnations of Simon [and other pharisees], and even the reproofs of my sister, [Martha]?"[70]

---

[70] This is a reference to the incident of a woman known to be a sinner washing the feet of Jesus in the house of Simon the Pharisee (Luke 7:36–50) and to Martha reproaching Mary for not assisting her in

After this, the apostle James arrived. Now, this was the James who was referred to as the brother of my Son, and he was remarkably similar to Him in appearance. With many tears, he exclaimed, "O, my Lord and master! Only one day ago, Your beloved face was very much like mine. But, alas, now the resemblance is entirely gone! Your hands and feet have been pierced with nails, and Your body has been wounded and bruised from the top of Your head to the soles of Your feet! Yet I remain completely unharmed." And he swore that he would take neither food nor drink until the likeness between my Son and himself had been restored.[71] All the disciples came and mourned deeply over the death of their master.

But then, it came about that the body of my deceased Son was miraculously restored! What immense consolation it brought to me and to all the disciples! In this glorified body, there were no wounds or scars to be seen, except for the five scars of the sacred wounds of His crucifixion. And these five wounds are destined to remain visibly on His body until the final Day of Judgment. But, apart from these, His body [although dead] appeared entirely healthy, as if He had never

---

domestic duties (Luke 10:38–42). Traditionally, these women were both identified with Mary Magdalene.

[71] This is consistent with the ancient tradition that the apostle James the Less swore not to eat or drink until he had seen the resurrected Lord.

undergone the ordeal of His passion. The consolation which the sight of this brought to us was truly immeasurable!

When the disciples wanted to place the body in a tomb, I was overcome with sadness. I embraced it firmly and could scarcely be induced to be separated from it. I spoke to the apostle John in desperation, saying, "Dearest John, leave me at least with my dead Son, Whom I am no longer able to possess alive! But if you really must place Him in a tomb, then please enclose me in that same tomb with Him so that I may be with him forever!"

John replied with great earnestness, "Beloved Lady, you know well that it cannot be otherwise than that the body of your Son is laid to rest amongst the dead. For the redemption of the entire race depends upon His most precious death!"

And so at last I granted permission for Him to be laid in the tomb. But as they laid Him in the tomb, I myself struggled to enter with Him. I threw myself upon the earth. My actions at this time were desperate and those of one who is maddened by grief. And all who looked on and saw my afflicted state were so moved that they shed tears too, not only for my deceased Son, but also on account of my own unspeakable agony.

Then Saint John wished to lead me back to the city under his filial care. But I resisted and sought to remain by the tomb and continue my lamentations. "Dear John," I implored, "do not separate me from my beloved Son! I wish to remain here at His resting place forever. Here I shall remain in mourning for Him until the very day that I die!" As I uttered this plea, all those present once again shared in my crying.

Nevertheless, John wisely sensed that my mind was quite overwhelmed and clouded with grief at this stage. So, gently but firmly, he took charge of me and led me from that place of sorrow back into the safety of the city. And when the crowds of people saw me once again, still clad in my garments bespotted with the precious blood of my Son, they cried out with a single voice, their hearts moved to sympathy at my miserable plight. They all said, "Oh, how great is the injustice and how dire the cruelty which has been done this day in Jerusalem to this most noble and lovely woman and to her innocent and holy Son!" And thus they took pity upon me.

But many of those who had persecuted and opposed Jesus still burned with envy and spite. Some of them seized Joseph [of Arimathea] in their malice and enclosed him—still alive—in the walls of Jerusalem. This was an act of mocking revenge for his kindness in respectfully entombing the body of Jesus. After some forty years had elapsed, when Titus and Vespasian laid siege to Jerusalem, they had the walls of the city demolished. And as this was being done—behold!—Joseph of Arimathea was discovered imprisoned within the walls, still living![72]

[During the time of my divine Son's passion, death, and burial, I seemed to hear a poignant song, sung from His most Sacred Heart to my own heart. It ran thus:]

> O Mother dear, behold My pain,
> As now I languish, bruised and slain;
> Behold the nails, the bloody dart
> Now thrust into My tender heart!
>
> They make Me drink of bitter wine,
> Whilst I in throes of death repine;
> The mocking and derisive word
> From scornful voices now is heard.
>
> The cross is raised unto the sky,
> Upon which now I soon must die;
> The earth now shakes, grows dark the sun
> As from this tree My blood does run.

---

[72] This strange and fantastical story seems to be entirely legendary in character and should not be read as historical truth in any way. During the Middle Ages, there were many and varied legends concerning Joseph of Arimathea in circulation, including that he went to Britain and that he was the mythical "wandering Jew." Such legends may be best appreciated as imaginative reflections on, and tributes to, the many relatively unknown disciples and supporters who played a role in the life of Christ of the early Church.

But, Mother, know My love for thee
Surpasses thine own love for Me;
I gaze on thee with tender care,
For thou My every pain dost share.[73]

In response to this plaintive and passionate lament, my own soul exclaimed, "Behold! The voice of my Beloved's blood calls out to me from the cross."

And from the depths of my heart, I cried out to my Son:

"O Jesus, my dearest one,
You have been made the scorn of humankind,
You, Who are acclaimed as the Lord of the angels!
Behold, O my heart, your Beloved!—
How His pale feet are pierced by nails.
See His body, not resting in comfort,
But stretched upon the horrid wood of the cross.

"O Jesus, You are the salvation of all the world!
O Jesus, my Beloved, You are the God of infinite glory,
Yet now You have become a contemptible worm in the sight of all.
O Jesus, You are the radiance of the angels;
You are the majesty and beauty of the Divinity!

---

[73] This passage is in rhyming verse in the original Latin. It has been freely adapted here to replicate the effect of the rhyme and meter of the original.

And You have ascended the tree of the cross.
Upon this cross, You have spread Your arms,
And poured forth Your precious blood—
Upon the grim tree of this dreadful cross
Now blooms the glowing, crimson flower of our
eternal salvation!"

Anselm: [My Lady Mary, truly you have shared with me
many wondrous things this day!]

What shall I repay the Lord for all He has given to me?
The cup of salvation I shall raise;
I will call upon the name of the Lord.[74]
Thanks be to God! Amen.

---

[74] Psalm 114:12–13.

THE BOOK OF THE
PASSION OF OUR LORD

*(An anonymous medieval Latin text traditionally
attributed to Saint Bernard of Clairvaux)*

1

Bernard: OF ALL THE beings either reigning in heaven above or wandering this earth below, which of them could possibly refrain from weeping when they hear of the dolorous tale of the passion of Our Lord? For in this saving passion, the one Who was Monarch of the angels was despised by mere mortals; the one Who was the true Son of God became the scorn of the people. Who could stop themselves from crying when they hear such bitter and heartrending things? What heart could be cold and stony enough to hold back its tears?

O Mary, my Mother and Queen, I know that you are now glorified beyond all measure in heaven! For just as you shared the bitter pain of the bloody nails which once affixed your divine Son to that dreaded cross, now you share with Him the perfect beatitude of His glorious resurrection. I ask you, my Lady, to permit me to share in those tears which you shed during the sufferings, passion, and death of your Son.

Pour into my heart the grace of such weeping, whereby my own heart may feel something of your own pain and sorrow, and therefore may merit—by God's grace—to share with you in the splendid glories of heaven.

Recall, O Mary, that very often I have conversed with you in prayer and that you have spoken to me frequently of the sorrows which you bore because of the death of your only-begotten Son. Speak to me, I implore you, of this once more.[1]

Mary: Do you really wish me to speak to you of these sorrowful events?

Bernard: Yes, such is my earnest desire. I must ask you, my Mother, to call to mind once more that bitterness of soul which afflicted you so grievously at that time. Let us converse on the events which transpired on that most dark and dreadful day. Tell me all that happened, the full series of events, with perfect and unconcealed truthfulness, for you yourself are the very Mother of Truth.

Mary: What you ask is a thing involving great distress and pain! But because I am now glorified with the divine splendor of the Resurrection, all my thoughts and feelings are pervaded with perfect and infinite bliss. Therefore, my

---

[1] The Latin text in this paragraph is somewhat confused and appears to contain errors and discontinuities. Fortunately, however, the general sense of it is fairly clear. The English rendering offered here has been freely adapted for the sake of communicating this sense.

heart can no longer be afflicted with sorrow; hence, in my glorified state, I shed no more tears. But you, Bernard, my son, shall surely be filled with weeping as you write these piteous and painful things.

Bernard: O Mary, I long to weep and to shed tears for the passion of your Son and to share with you something of the bitter sorrows which you then felt. I long for my sinful heart to be pierced as your own sinless and Immaculate Heart once was! Truly, nothing shall bring greater benefit to my soul. Grant me, my Lady, the favor I humbly ask of you.

Mary: Very well, so be it. Listen carefully, Bernard, to my words.

Bernard: My Lady, were you in Jerusalem when your Son was captured and arrested? Were you there when He was bound with chains and led before the high priest, Ananias?

Mary: I was indeed present in Jerusalem at that time. When I heard that He had been arrested, I rushed as fast as my steps could carry me, filled with tears. I beheld Him there, being struck cruel blows with the fists of the guards and being slapped without mercy. They were spitting upon His dear face and had placed a grotesque crown of thorns upon His head, treating Him as if He were an object of disgrace and contempt. How my heart trembled within me as I saw it! My spirit almost failed me, so much so that I was totally incapable of uttering a sound. It was as if all my senses were darkened, and I feinted away.

There were with me at that time my sisters and many other women. These also wept for my Son, as if He were their only-begotten child too. Amongst these women was Mary Magdalene. And she was afflicted with grief beyond all the others, except myself alone.

My Son, the Messiah and true God, was then taken forth at the command of Pilate. A herald stood by proclaiming the sentence which had been passed against Him. Jesus came out, carrying His own cross and walking with faltering steps towards the place of His execution. And a great multitude were then present, following Him as well. Some of these mourned for Him and deplored the unjust and horrendous punishment which awaited Him. But many others went with the crowd also, mocking and deriding Him without mercy. I, His mother, followed my Son as closely as possible, together with a group of faithful women from Galilee. These all wept with sincere pity and compassion. Thus my divine Child made His painful and lugubrious way to the grim hill of Calvary.

2

[Mary continues her discourse to Bernard.]

THEN, BEFORE MY very eyes, I saw my beloved Child raised up on the cross and fixed to its hard wood with piercing and unrelenting nails. All the while, He remained like a gentle lamb in the presence of its shearers, not uttering a word nor opening His mouth. Thus I, the handmaid of the Lord, looked upon my Master being tortured! Thus I, the Mother of God, saw my Son hanging from the cross, dying in the throngs of a shameful and ignominious death. The pain and agony which tore through my heart then was so intense that no words could ever express it! His blood gushed forth from the four wounds He then bore—upon each of His hands and feet, where the nails had penetrated His holy flesh. As a crimson flood, His precious blood poured onto the wood of the cross and covered the iron of the nails.

The rare and unique beauty which had hitherto been so wonderfully visible upon His face was now entirely concealed and distorted by His wounds, the outflow of blood and the agony which He felt. He had always been, as the Psalm eloquently expresses it, "One beautiful beyond the sons of mortals."[2] Yet now He displayed neither beauty nor grace. And thus I understood to be fulfilled that prophetic oracle, that "he had no form or comeliness, and when we looked upon him, there was nothing of beauty to attract us."[3]

Indeed, the bruises on His face from the cruel blows which had been inflicted upon Him made Him hardly recognizable. It was almost as if I had been deprived of that Son of mine of uniquely beautiful and noble appearance, Whom I had carried in my womb and to Whom I had given birth. He had been my one Child and my only-begotten Son, and in Him alone I had placed all my hopes and all my love. The anguish and sorrow which came over me were so oppressive and total that my poor heart was scarcely able to contain them without bursting!

My speech failed me entirely, and the only sounds which I could produce were sighs and wailings. I wished then to speak—to offer some words of consolation, or to pour out some prayer to heaven. But my pain totally suppressed my faculty of speech. For whenever I conceived some word

---

[2] Psalm 44:2.
[3] Isaiah 52:3.

or utterance in my mind and heart, my mouth could not articulate it. For love and pain so overpowered my tongue and mouth that I could utter no intelligible words but only the groans and sighs of sheer desperation, expressing an anguish and sorrow entirely beyond mortal speech.

3

[Mary continues her discourse to Bernard.]

YET, THOUGH I had been rendered incapable of speech, I continued to gaze intently upon my beloved Son dying on the cross. He strove to offer words of consolation to me. For He saw me weeping, and His compassionate heart sought to console me, even in the midst of His own agony. But at this point, nothing at all could bring me any alleviation of my grief.

I spoke by weeping, and I wept by speaking. While a wordless lament of infinite bitterness poured forth from my lips, my heart thus proclaimed:

> O my Son, my only Son! How I wish that I could die for You! If You, my Son, die like this, why should not I, Your mother, also be permitted to die? My one Beloved, do not depart from me

like this; do not leave me alone. Rather, draw me to Yourself so that I may die with You! O Death, do not spare me from your merciful embrace! As you clutch my dear Son from me, take me also, I implore you!

My Son, You are the one joy of my life and the very desire of my soul! Let me die with You now, on this black and baleful day. Grant this favor to me, who bore You into this world, only so that You would die on a cross. Have pity upon me, and draw me to Yourself on this infernal gallows so that we may die as one flesh, even as we shared one heart and one love!

O Death, in taking my Son, you are taking the sole ray of light which illuminates this dark world! In stealing from me my Son, you take away my joy; nay, more than this, you take my very life, my sweetness, and my hope! Why should the Mother live when the Son is no more? You have not spared my Child; do not spare me! O merciful Death, come to me as my consolation and savior!

At that time, O Bernard, I was speaking quite irrationally, overcome by the madness of grief and pain. Yet, in truth, I should have been very glad to have died at that time and to have found sweet relief in oblivion. But the death for which I then longed fled from me. For death would have been less bitter to me than witnessing the death of my beloved Son.

Then, overcome with emotion, I managed to speak aloud to Jesus. I said to Him:

> O my dearest Child! You are to me a father and a mother; You are to me my spouse and my Son. You were truly everything to me! And now I lose my father and my mother, my spouse and my Son! Everything I have and everything I am is taken away from me. Where shall I go? To whom shall I turn?

> My Son, I know that You are true God and that all things are possible to You. If You do not wish to take me with You as You die, I beg You at least to give me some wise counsel or some word which shall bring me consolation and fortitude.

4

[Mary continues her discourse to Bernard.]

THEN, BERNARD, I noticed that my Son turned His divine eyes to the apostle John, who also stood by the cross. My Son opened His mouth and spoke to me. Indicating John with His eyes, He said, "Woman, behold your son!"[4] John, the youngest of the apostles, then bore a downcast and melancholy countenance and was crying silent tears of deep grief.

But Jesus said to him:

> O gentle youth, why are you so weak and so prone to weeping and mourning? For you know that I came into the world to undergo this very suffering. You know that I assumed human flesh so that I could bear the horrors of the cross and thus save the human race from perdition. How else, I ask you, may the eternal words of Scripture be fulfilled?

---

[4] John 19:26.

Often have I told you that the Son of Man must suffer and die for the salvation of humankind, but that I shall rise again on the third day and appear openly to you and to all the disciples. Cease to weep! Put aside your mourning, for now I go to My heavenly Father. Yes, I ascend to receive the glory of My paternal heritage, which is nothing less than the majesty of the Divinity! You should not weep for Me but rather congratulate Me and rejoice with Me. For I have now found the sheep that was lost—which is to say, I have now rescued the souls of the children of Adam from the sentence of eternal damnation. One man now dies so that the entire world may be saved!

O beloved John, does it behoove you to be displeased at that which is pleasing to God the Father? Or is it your wish that I should not drink of the chalice which my eternal Father has given to Me to drink?

Then, turning to me once more, Jesus spoke to me words of consolation and encouragement, saying:

Neither should you weep now, My sweetest Mother! For I am not deserting you. I do not abandon you. I am with you now, and I shall be with you for all ages! Although I perish now according to the mortal flesh, in My divine nature I remain the one Who was, Who is, and Who ever shall be. Through this Divinity, I am not subject to death, for I am immortal. Through this divine nature, I am afflicted by no suffering, for I am impassible. You yourself, as My Mother, know well from whence I have come and to where I now go. For, indeed, it is the time that I return to the One who sent Me. Where I now go, you are not able yet to follow. But you shall certainly follow me after this![5]

"My disciple, John, who has hitherto been a nephew to you, will henceforth be regarded as your son. He shall take good care of you and will offer you consolation, support, and care most lovingly and faithfully." And then He directed His gaze to John and said to him, "Behold, your mother![6] You are henceforth to serve and protect her diligently. Accept My beloved Mother into your care. Care for her as if she were your very own mother, or rather, care for her, because she is My own immaculate Mother, and therefore the true Mother of God!"

---

[5]   See John 13:36.
[6]   John 19:27.

(Translator's note: From this point onwards, the text seems to cease to be part of Mary's discourse, as it consistently refers to her in the third person. On the other hand, it is no longer framed as an address of Bernard to Mary. It seems that the author or scribe at this point departed from his original plan of composing his work in the form of a dialogue.)

THESE TWO VIRGINS, Mary and John,[7] both stood in mute silence. Indeed, because of the profound grief they each felt, they were quite unable to speak. They looked upon Christ, Whom they both loved so dearly, as one virtually dead. They each also felt as if they were dead and could hardly breathe, much less speak. Their spirits utterly failed them. They felt nothing except for grief and pain. They expressed

---

7   Saint John is traditionally identified as being a virgin. Most ancient authorities describe him as being very young and unmarried when he became a follower of Christ.

their love for their crucified Lord with weeping, and they wept for Him with the deepest of love. And the bitter sword of sorrow, and the cruel dagger of grief, pierced the hearts of each of them. Yet the pain of Mary was the greater of the two, for she loved Jesus as only a mother may love. Indeed, she felt each of the wounds on the body of Christ as if they were her own wounds. She felt the spear which pierced the side of Christ as much (or more) as if it had been thrust into her own side. In dying, Christ bore on Himself the entire debt of all the sins of humankind, but a heavier and bitterer burden for Him at that time was to witness the agony of His own beloved Mother's soul.

At this point, Christ spoke to both His Mother and the apostle John. "I thirst," He said. And those who had crucified Him offered Him a foul concoction of vinegar mixed with gall.[8] After this, He exclaimed, "It is consummated!" and cried out in a loud voice, "Father, into Your hands I commend My spirit." And, saying this, He breathed His last.

> At this, the earth did quake,
> The land commenced to shake,
> The sun withheld its light,
> The sky grew black as night.

---

[8] See Matthew 27:34.

The rocks were split apart,
And trembled, too, each heart,
And, lo, the holy dead
Were from their graves then led.

What plenitude of woe
The whole earth then did know!
The boundless welkin cries,
As God's true Son now dies.

6

CONSIDER, O READER, just how much pain the holy Mother of God felt at that most dire of times. For she was more noble and innocent than any other woman who ever lived, and therefore more sensitive to feelings of any kind. No tongue is able to express the depths of her sorrows, nor is any mind able to imagine the bitterness which Mary then experienced. She stood immobile by the cross, as if she herself had been frozen by the cold touch of death whilst she looked upon the one Whom she had conceived by the Holy Spirit and Whom she bore as an inviolate Virgin. What torments and extremities of pain her tender and Immaculate Heart felt!

Her agony was so great that she was like one who was herself dead. Her face assumed the ghostly pallor of a corpse. Yet somehow she was unable to die, although she fervently desired death. Thus while yet living, she died; yet in thus dying, she still lived.

So she waited for the body of her beloved Child to be taken down from the cross and deposited in her arms. And, through her tears, she cried out to the guards and soldiers, "You have completed now your ignominious and impious task! Now give to me the body of my Son, that we may be united in death; so that, just as He has now perished, so may the infinite pain of my grief also perish; and so that, just as the spark of His mortal life has been consigned to the darkness of oblivion, so may my pain feel the blank embrace of nothingness. Give Him to me so that His body may serve as my support and my consolation, for though His life is gone, yet my love for Him remains!"

Thus stood Mary, by the cross her mournful station keeping. With infinite love and compassion, she gazed upon the adorable and noble face of her Son, hanging from the wood of the cross, suspended from that fierce and fateful tree. And she fell to her knees and embraced its hard surface warmly. And where its wood had been stained by the blood of Christ, she kissed it passionately, as if she were kissing and embracing her dear Child Himself. Indeed, it is the nature of love to hope for much, to hope even for that which is impossible!

And she stretched out her hands to reach the lifeless body of Christ, but, alas, He was beyond her reach. So she raised herself up, stretching her body that she might touch Him. Yet she could not reach Him, and, in her exertions, she stumbled to the ground. And there, overcome by despair and oppressed by hopeless grief, she lay prostrate, as if crushed by the sheer immensity of her anguish. Yet the force of love still burned ardently within her, and this fought against her despair. This force of love—divine and insuperable—then raised her up once more. Her hand reached out to her Son, yet He remained beyond her reach. Her face and cheeks were pale with deathly whiteness, yet her lips shone forth crimson, stained by the precious blood of her Son from her kissing of His cross. And as each drop of His divine blood spilt upon the ground, she would kiss it with all the fervor of maternal love and holy longing.

7

MEANWHILE, A CERTAIN noble man, Joseph by name, who was a disciple of Christ, although a secret one,[9] betook himself to see Pilate. Approaching him with full confidence, he requested that he be given the body of Jesus. Pilate agreed to this and gave him permission to take the body and bury it as he saw fit. Joseph then went to see another secret disciple of Christ, Nicodemus, who was a respected expert in the Jewish law. Together they made for the place where their Lord had been crucified, bringing with them suitable tools for taking the body from the cross. With these they removed the nails, then gently took Christ from the Tree of Death upon which He hung.

As Mary saw them doing this, her spirits were somewhat strengthened, and she raised herself like a dead woman coming back to life. She offered to assist Joseph and

---

[9] See Matthew 27:57.

Nicodemus, as much as she was able. And she herself drew out one of the nails, which had been driven through one of His hands, from the body of her Son. She also helped by supporting His body while the other nails were being drawn out, lest it should fall to the ground.

Once the first hand of her Son had been loosened from the cross, Mary clasped it lovingly to her heart. And when His whole body was taken down, she embraced it and covered it with tender kisses. As she held Him to herself firmly, the pangs of grief were renewed in her. Holding her Son in a silent embrace, she sat immobile, as if transfixed again by the sword of sorrow, or like one frozen by the chill winds of death.

She then took the noble head of her deceased Son to herself. Her tears poured forth in a ceaseless stream, running over the face of Christ. How eagerly did she kiss Him on the forehead, the cheeks, the eyes, and the nose! So great was her flow of tears then that one would have believed her entire being, body and soul, to have been liquefied and to be issuing forth in rivulets from her eyes. Her tears covered the entire body of Christ, mingling with the stains of blood which were upon it.

And some of these tears fell onto the large stone on which she held her lifeless Son. Such was the bitterness and mystical potency of these tears that they left marks upon the hard stone. And to this very day, the marks where these tears of the Virgin fell may still be seen upon that ancient rock on the desolate hill of Calvary.

Who was this One for whom the Blessed Mary then mourned so grievously? He was her only-begotten Son, whom she had conceived as a Virgin and to whom she had given birth without pain. He was, to her, her all and her everything; He was not only her Son but also her very Lord and God. And in seeing His dead body, she beheld not only the death of a single human being but the death of her divine Lord.

If anyone is able, let them describe to me the bitterness of the sorrow which then pierced her most tender and Immaculate Heart! But I do not believe that her pain may ever be truly or adequately described. Nevertheless, her grief, while immense and inconceivable, did not become impious despair. For despair implies a lack of hope, and a lack of hope implies a lack of faith. Although Mary's tears flowed without restraint and although her agony of grief was unbounded, yet still she believed (or rather, knew) deep within her heart that her Son would rise again gloriously from the tomb on the third day.

8

A SMALL GROUP of holy women also remained weeping and lamenting, out of the much larger gathering who had been there earlier. A very small number of men were there too, who mourned for Christ together with His Virgin Mother. There were present also angels amongst them. Indeed, these angels wept, insofar as angels are able to weep. It may be said that they wept and rejoiced simultaneously. For they felt deep compassion at the death of the most innocent Son of God, yet they rejoiced to know that the salvation of the human race had thereby been accomplished.

As I judge it, what perturbed the minds of these angels most deeply was to witness the extremity of grief which Mary displayed and to recognize the sorrow which had penetrated her maidenly and innocent heart. Oh, who, even of the angels and archangels, would not have wept at this piteous sight! If anyone objects that it is contrary to nature for the angels to have wept, I would reply that it was no less contrary to nature for the divine Christ—Who was immortal God—to have died. Those angels beheld the ever-living Son of God to lie dead, wounded, and tortured by the wicked. They beheld His glorious ever-Virgin Mother to be crushed and tormented by grief—she who was eternally pre-destined to be the Mother of God, the most blessed, merciful, pure, beautiful, holy, and sweet fruit of all Creation. She wept with a poignancy which taught the very angels, those beings of pure spirit, how to weep! Indeed, I should wonder very greatly if the angels did not then weep, even though they dwell in an immutable celestial beatitude in which weeping is impossible. I argue that, if it was possible for the deathless and immortal Deity, through the human flesh He had assumed, to die, then it is equally possible for the blessed and impassible angels, through the death of Jesus and the tears of Mary, to have cried.

Then Joseph of Arimathea, that just and holy man who, together with Nicodemus, had removed the body of Christ from the cross, now wrapped it in a clean sheet scented with precious aromas, as the Gospel testifies.[10] He lovingly and reverently placed it in a new tomb, which had been constructed for his own burial. Then, legions of angels—myriads of myriads—all gathered at the tomb to sing the exequys of their eternal King. Invisible to mortal eyes and

---

[10] John 19:39.

unheard by mortal ears, these poured forth their glorious praises to Christ. Their mellifluous strains ascended to the very vault of heaven, splendid and beautiful in the glowing radiance of transcendent and celestial harmony.

And Mary herself stood by the tomb, pouring forth heartrending dirges and lamentations through the tears which she continued to cry. And even as her cherished Son was taken to the tomb, she continued to cling to Him and cover Him with warm, insistent kisses, embracing Him with the love which only a mother may know or understand. And incessantly she repeated her humble supplication, "Have mercy on me, O Lord. Have mercy on me!"

And she spoke to Joseph of Arimathea and those who assisted him, saying, "Permit me to embrace the body of my darling Son for a little while, I implore you! In this way, I shall find a trace of consolation. I may gaze into His tender face and kiss Him a little more. Do not consign Him so hastily to the tomb, but give His glorious body, now lifeless and broken, to me, His wretched Mother! But if you must now place Him in the tomb, then bury me with Him!"

And thus it was that as these disciples placed the body of Christ in the tomb, His Mother clung to Him desperately. For she wished to retain her beloved Son for herself, but the disciples knew that He had to be decently buried. Thus there arose a dispute between them, although both were motivated by nothing but the purest of piety and devotion. The dispute continued for some time, and the anguish which Joseph of Arimathea felt at the lamentation of Mary almost exceeded the grief they felt for Christ Himself.[11]

---

[11] The translation offered here has here been slightly abridged. The Latin text continues in this vein at some length, describing the conflict between Mary, who resisted the attempts to entomb Christ, and Joseph and the other disciples, who realized that it was necessary and proper for His body to be buried. Obviously, Mary is still overwhelmed with grief at this stage.

9

IT WAS THE apostle Saint John, to whom Christ had commended the care and protection of His Mother, who was at last able to resolve this situation. He approached Mary respectfully and tenderly and was able raise her up and to separate her from her determined clinging to the body of her Son. Though Mary continued to weep bitterly, she was utterly fatigued from her mourning and from the intensity of her grief. John gently led her into Jerusalem, together with the other women who accompanied her. And as she entered the city, a great multitude of women joined her in procession, weeping just as she wept. For they were moved to sorrow not only by the unjust death of the divine Son but also by the bitter grief of the holy Mother.

In truth, anyone who witnessed this scene would have scarcely been able to withhold their own tears. For she wept so reverently and so touchingly that whoever beheld her was also moved to weeping, whether willingly or unwillingly. Hence it came about that the whole city of Jerusalem resounded with uncontrollable lamentations and wails, and that all its streets were flooded with tears.

Blessed Mary wept, and all who accompanied her wept too. Eventually, the Mother of God arrived at the house of John. And there she remained, enclosed in secret, for some time. And John cared for her with the utmost devotion and solicitude, as if she were his very own Mother. And Mary came to love John in her heart, as if he were her very own son.

O happy and blessed John! For the Lord Himself commended to you His most precious treasure—Mary, His immaculate and gracious Mother. Thus did He reward you for your particular love towards Him. And you continued to express this love for Jesus through the love which you bore to His glorious Mother.

Saint John, you were wondrously blessed by Christ, and you were doubly blessed through His holy Mother, whom you loved with a devout and pure heart! Blessed, indeed, are all who love Mary, the glorious, ever-Virgin Mother of our God and Lord, Jesus Christ, who reigns with the Father and the Holy Spirit, God forever and ever. Amen.

OUR LADY'S LAMENT

*(An anonymous Middle English text
attributed to John Lydgate)*

I, MARY, THE Mother of Jesus, sat in Jerusalem on the holy feast of Passover,[1] alone in my house, for a great multitude of people then crowded the city because of the festivity. I closed my doors and sat alone, as was my custom. The private thoughts of my heart all went out to my dear Son Jesus, where He might be and what He might be doing. For towards Him was all my love and all my desire directed; I earnestly longed to see Him and hoped that in the evening before the feast of the Passover He would come.

And I sat occupied in praying my devotions and waited for His arrival longingly. And then suddenly, after the sun had set, I heard a great tumult of the people in the street outside. They were crying out as if they had been seized with frenzy. But I, Mary, sitting by myself alone, knew not the

---

[1] The original Middle English text uses the word "Easter" here, but to most modern readers this would seem distinctly anachronistic. As the words "Pasch" and "Easter" were treated as synonyms in Middle English, it is clear that the word "Easter" is used by the author to signify Passover.

cause of their great crying out and the commotion which had arisen. I said to myself, "Would to God that I were now with my sweet Son Jesus! Who shall tell me tidings of my dear Child? For I dread that some disaster has befallen Him, for I have heard for a few days now that there are many who are conspiring to kill Him."

And when I, Mary, sorrowful and fearfully aghast, spoke to myself in this manner, I looked around, hoping that one of His apostles might bring to me some tidings of my sweet Son. Then I heard at that moment suddenly someone knocking at my door. And I arose at once and ran to the window of my chamber and looked out. There I saw Mary Magdalene, clothed in the black garments of mourning. She appeared as if she had been weeping, and her hair was all disheveled. She looked up at me and said, "Come down to me, most devout of all women, for I have tidings of thy Son!"

And then I, Mary, smitten with the sword of sorrow, went down and opened the door. And the devout Mary Magdalene spoke to me and said, "O Mary, most reverend mother of all women, have you perchance heard the new tidings of Jesus, thy sweet Son and my own revered Master?"

At this, I became anxious and alarmed. At once I replied to her, full of sorrow and concern, asking, "Do *you* know anything of these new tidings of my sweet Son?" And then Magdalene, weeping bitterly, spoke to me these words, "Jesus, thy Son and thy love, and my own Master too, has now been taken prisoner! He has been cruelly and wickedly bound with cords. Yes, they have arrested Him, beaten Him, and dragged Him away!" And when I, Mary, Jesus's mother, heard these words, I was again painfully smitten with the bitter sword of sorrow through my poor heart.

At this point, I collapsed to the ground like a dead woman. When Mary Magdalene had brought me this news of my Son's arrest, it was the beginning of the night. Such horrendous darkness came about me then that I knew not where to go, and I had no one to assist or comfort me. And so I lay all that night upon the earth weeping, and all my house was wet with the tears which flowed from my eyes. Then I opened my heart in plaintive and supplicant prayer, crying out desperately to God, "O Holy Father, I wonder why didst Thou ever cause me to become a mother and bestow upon me a child? For now I am bereaved of this child and left utterly alone. I feel no longer the most blessed but rather the most sorrowful of all women!"

Then I directed my lamentation to the archangel Gabriel, saying, "O Gabriel, why didst thou greet me thus if thy greeting has brought to me this extremity of sorrow? Behold now, O Gabriel, instead of the joy that thy salutation brought me, now I have pain, and instead of the gladness I felt then, now I have sorrow. I am bereaved of my only-begotten Child! Instead of honor, I have shame, and instead of life, I have death! And instead of the heavenly blessing that thou didst bring me then, now a dark curse of melancholy has fallen upon me!"

And then I said unto myself, "O, unhappy and afflicted maiden and most sorrowful of mothers! Why didst thou conceive a child and bear an infant, only to be so wickedly bereaved of this dearest Son of thine?" And with such words, and with much weeping and sorrow and lamentation and grinding of teeth, I spent that entire night, until the dawn arose in the east. Then the darkness little by little gave way to light, and the sun shone upon the earth. Alas, then sprang the most dreadful of all days for me!

And then stood I up from the ground, like a dead body arising by some ghostly power. Now, there were at that time in Jerusalem a number of devout women from Galilee who had spent the whole night in a vigil of prayer in the Temple. When these women had heard that my sweet Son had been arrested and cruelly bound by the servants of the high priests, they all hastened to visit me, His sorrowful mother, and to bring me such comfort as they could.

I then addressed Mary Magdalene, my sisters, and these holy women from Galilee, saying to them, "Let us go forth, my sisters, so that we might see my son, Jesus! Verily, He is the only comfort in my life."

And although my body was feeble and weak from the sufferings I had endured that night on account of my anxiety and sorrow for my sweet son, Jesus, these holy women faithfully supported me on their arms. And thus we were able to venture forth in search of my dear Child.

As we made our way through the streets of Jerusalem, we met with some of His disciples, who were weeping bitterly. I spoke and asked them, "Have you seen my dear Son? If so, tell me, I beseech you, where it was that you last saw His face?"

They continued to weep but replied to my question thus, "We saw Him cruelly bound with cords and beaten with scourges! We saw His holy face wretchedly befouled with spittle, and Him being led forth by the wicked minions of Caiaphas. And we saw Him handed over to the governor, Pilate. When we last beheld Him, His countenance was deathly pale, and His speech was ghostly. All His body seemed utterly changed so that we scarcely could know Him!"

And then I, Mary, Jesus's mother, most sorrowful of all mothers, uttered these words in my anguish, "O Jesus, my sweet Son, what is it that I hear now of Thee? What bitter and hard tidings are now revealed to me?"

And then I addressed the disciples again, asking, "Is there any way that I may see my sweet Son, Jesus, so that I might rescue Him from the hands of His captors?" And, seeing my sorrow, some of them said to me, "Go, Lady, and tarry not if you would see thy Son alive once more! For He is now being led with armed knights to Pilate's palace, for the priests of the Temple all plot to have Him sentenced to a most horrendous death." And when I, Mary, heard these words, I was smitten again through my heart with sorrow.

As a dead woman, I went forth, borne up by my sisters. Indeed, I could scarcely manage the journey to Pilate's palace for very faintness and weakness, even with their kind support. When I finally arrived there, it was the third hour of the day. Once there, I willingly would have gone into the palace at once, yet I could not draw near to the gates because of the very great multitude of people assembled there. But I came as near as I could and stood there as still as a stone planted in the earth. I then raised up my eyes to see through the windows of the palace, hoping to be able to catch some glimpse of my sweet Son, Jesus. And, lo, Pilate himself came to the window of the palace and said to all the great multitude of people assembled there, "I find there to be no case against Jesus. He has done naught which would merit punishment, much less the sentence of death. Now, ye all know well that it be my custom to release to you a prisoner at this time of festival. Do you wish me to release this innocent man, Jesus, or would you prefer that I give you the known homicide, Barabbas?"

And when I, Mary, heard him say this, I was filled with hope! I lifted up my head as though I had risen from death to life. For truly, I fully expected that Barabbas, the notorious killer, should have been put to death, and that my Son, Jesus, would be let go alive. But then, alas, I heard the horrible noise of all the people crying out for His blood. They demanded vociferously, "Do Jesus unto death on a cross! Crucify Him!" And when I heard this vicious and bloodthirsty crying out of the people, I was smitten yet again through my heart with the sword of sorrow.

As a dead woman, I then fell down upon the earth, seeming to the people as though I had expired. And there I lay motionless for some time, till my sisters gathered me up and comforted me. And so I stood there long and patiently, waiting in the hope that I might have seen my sweet Son, Jesus, again. I hoped also to have had the opportunity to speak with Pilate and to implore him earnestly that he release to me my sweet Son, Jesus, that meek and innocent Lamb of God!

But the wicked Pharisees and scribes, when they heard me cry and saw me weeping so very grievously, were not in the least touched with pity or compassion. Rather, they reproached me harshly, saying, "Hold thy peace, thou mother of a thief and nourisher of this traitor! For thy Son is deserving of death, for He is beguiling the common people and leading them astray. Therefore thou shalt see Him done to death on the cross before thy very own eyes!" And then I fell down once more as a woman in despair, being thus despised and insulted by all. Meanwhile, the crowds continued to cry out as though they had been possessed by some demon of cruel frenzy and hellish malice, saying, "Bring out Jesus of Nazareth to us, that He may be crucified, and done to death upon a cross!"

And so Pilate eventually assented to them. First, he had Him beaten with scourges and then clothed Him in mocking purple. After this, he handed Him over to be crucified. And then they brought Him forth, before the eyes of me, His most wretched mother. I beheld Jesus, my sweet Son, crowned with a crown of thorns upon His head, and His eyes all pale, and His face all red from blood. And He bore upon His back the heavy cross on which He was to die. He had a cord about His neck, as if He were a common criminal, and He was put between two convicted thieves.

And when I saw this cruel sight, then all my strength utterly failed me. Sorrow flared up in my heart with renewed bitterness, and my anguish almost suffocated me. Yet such a great crowd pressed around my dear Son that I could not approach Him, nor could He hear my voice because of all the clamor of the people. And then one of the holy women who accompanied me said, "Lady Mary, let us go by another route, and then we shall meet thy Son further along the way. That way, thou shalt have the chance to meet Him and speak to Him before His execution."

Upon hearing this prudent counsel, I promptly sprung up as a woman strengthened with a new spirit. We went swiftly along the suggested byway, and suddenly I met with my Son as He walked along, bearing the cross upon His back. And said I then these words to my sweet Son, Jesus, "O, my sweet Son, Jesus, whither goest Thou so swiftly and so heavily burdened with this Thy cruel cross? What then dost Thou wish to become of Thy poor mother? Will Thou leave me thus alone in despair—would Thou forsake me by hastening onwards to Thy death? O, my sweet Son, Jesus, give to me, Thy mother, Thy heavy cross, and I shall bear it on my back for Thee! And, my Son, do not presume to die without Thy mother, but, my sweet Child, let us die together even as we have lived, united always by love."

And then my sweet Son was touched more by my own manifest sorrow and despair than for the wounds and scourges which He felt Himself, and suffered more from my pain than from His own. Overcome with this compassion, He at once fell to the ground. And I, perceiving His sufferings, likewise fell to the ground, overwhelmed with grief. And I lay like a woman who has given up the ghost and is dead. But the people mercilessly dragged us both up. My Son was forced to arise and continue carrying the burden of His cross; while the wicked Pharisees seized me and violently dragged me away from my dear Child, Jesus.

And the cruel crowds, perceiving that my Son would soon fail from weakness, forced a man called Simon to bear the weight of the cross for Him, until they arrived near that dreaded place called Calvary. And there they savagely kicked

Him and smote with whips, forcing Him to take up the cross once more and to carry it upon His back up the Mount of Calvary. Thus the rabid and diabolic mob offered up to death the spotless Lamb of God—the One without Whom nothing else could exist[2]—my own sweet Son, Jesus!

And then I, Mary, most sorrowful of all mothers, followed after my sweet Son, Jesus, as fast as I could to witness the dolorous death that He, the Lamb of God and my own solace and joy, was destined to suffer. But scarcely did I have the strength to go to the Mount of Calvary, unless my sisters were supporting me. So worn and weary was my body that by the time I had arrived there, the wicked men had already cruelly affixed my Son to the cross and raised up that tree of death and planted it in the earth.

And then looked I upon my Son, Jesus, with tear-filled eyes, bitterly weeping and crying. And I said to Him these words; "O, my sweet Son, Jesus! O, my most beloved Jesus! Why, why lookest Thou not to me, Thy sorrowful and grieving mother? Why dost Thou turn thine eyes away? Why dost Thou leave me thus alone? O, whither shall I go, my sweet Son; where shall my heart find rest, my dearest Child ? O, since Thou hast no pity for Thyself, have pity on Thy sorrowful Mother!"

But when my sweet Son Jesus heard me speak in such a mournful and disconsolate manner, He said to me these

---

[2] See John 1:3.

words of consolation, "Woman, be thou of good comfort! For it is for this reason that I have come into the world; and for this reason it is that I took this body from thee, that hangs here on the cross today. For only thus may the human soul be redeemed from its servitude to the world and the devil, and only thus may souls that were lost to sin be saved. Yes, it is for that reason alone that I suffer this cruel and bitter passion that thou dost behold.

"And therefore, O Mother, cease from thy weeping and thy crying; for this is my heavenly Father's will. My Mother, let it also be *thy* will, for in my death I shall slay death! And know that, with the victory of my passion, I shall arise again on the third day. And, therefore, Mother, I give you here to John, my disciple whom I love well. Let him be as a son to thee, and be thou as a mother unto him. And thee I entrust to him that he might protect and guard thee, for later do I die upon this cross!"

And when my Son, Jesus, had spoken these words, He raised up His eyes to heaven and commended His soul to His eternal Father. And thus, with a great cry, He yielded up His spirit. And then I, Mary, fell down to the earth, utterly overwhelmed with sorrow; and, such was my collapse that many of those present thought that I also had died.

And at about the ninth hour,[3] there came a host of cruel centurions and armed knights. These stood before my son,

---

[3] 3:00 p.m.

and one of them with a spear opened His side and cleft His heart in two. And when my precious Son's side was thus then opened and His sacred heart split in two, the knights then went their way and departed.

And then came Joseph of Arimathea, a nobleman possessing a righteous and just heart. This Joseph wished earnestly and piously to take off the cross the deceased body of my Son, Jesus. When I saw him, my spirit returned to me, and I took new strength and roused myself from the stupor of my grief. I spoke to him thus, "O, my good Joseph! O, my dear, and worthy Joseph! Is it thy intention to take down from this hateful cross the body of my sweet Son, Jesus?"

And Joseph replied to me full of courteous and respect, "O Mary, holy Mother of Jesus, who was also the Son of God and the Son of heaven! O Mother and Virgin, and gentle maiden without stain of guilt of sin! Abide here a little while, I beseech thee. Cease from thy weeping and thy sorrow; for I know that thou art the most blessed among women, and I believe without any doubt that thy Son, Jesus, will arise from death to life in a very short time! Therefore, noble Lady, now in the meanwhile let us bury His holy body in a right worthy manner. For tomorrow is a most solemn Sabbath, and we are not permitted to do any work then."

When Joseph had said these words to me, I was somewhat comforted by them. I helped to wash my Son's body, for it had been much befouled by spitting, beating, bruising, and bleeding. And when we had washed it, we arranged it for burial and anointed it. At this, I was again smitten with a new and most bitter sorrow!

And then I said these words to my sweet Son, where He lay dead, "O Thou most pure and holy Body that liest here, why didst Thou thus die upon the cross and be offered up as a ransom for our foul sins? For truly Thou art most holy and sacred and completely free from sin, and sin has no claim upon Thee and Thou hast naught to do with sin! And yet Thou hast grievously borne the sins of all by Thy precious blood and by Thy dire pains and by Thy most bitter death."

And when I had said these words, I fell down upon the body of my sweet Son, Jesus, weeping bitterly and crying disconsolately. Then I kissed the wounds of His head and of His hands and of His feet, and the wound in His side, and then I clasped all the body in my arms and kissed it. And I spoke also these words, "O, my sweet Son, Jesus, I, Thy wretched mother, did not expect to see Thee suffer and die thus! Nor did I expect the sorrows that I have suffered for Thee.[4] But much more I believe myself to have been blessed with a unique and singular joy in being Thy

---

[4]   This should not be understood as contradicting the prophecy of Simon in Luke 2:35, or suggesting that Mary was not mindful of it. For although the Blessed Virgin was certainly aware that her Son would suffer and that she also would suffer on His account, she was not necessarily aware in advance of the exact kind or extent of the sufferings that He (and she) would undergo.

mother, and had hoped never to have been separated from Thee for all eternity!"

And while I uttered these words of pain and desperation, Joseph with his companions moved swiftly to wind and to bind my Son in his burial sheet. But when they had bound a part of His body and were about to bind another, I fell down to the wounds that were bound and strove to unbind them again. For I was smitten with a fresh wave of sorrow so that, for a long time, I refused to permit them to bind up His body. But despite all the lamentations and wailings that I made, all those that were there took the body of my sweet Son, Jesus, out of my clasping hands so that, at last, they could bear Him away to the sepulcher.

As they did this, I followed closely, with inconsolable weeping and free-flowing tears. And when they came to His sepulcher, they would have interred Him there at once, but I refused to permit them to do so. Rather, I meekly implored them in a piteous manner, saying, "O you noble men and ye holy women, bury not my dear Son, Jesus, just yet, but allow me to hold Him a little while longer in mine arms, that I may kiss Him for the last time."

And when they saw the grave sorrow and dire distress that I was in, they took pity and made great lamentation and permitted me to embrace His body for a little while. But at last they felt that they needed to proceed with the entombment without further tarrying or delay. Then I,

Mary, wept anew. In my anguish, I cried out, "Bury me with Him, for verily I cannot live without Him!"

But then Joseph of Arimathea and his companions reverently but firmly separated me from the sepulcher. And they buried my sweet Son, Jesus, with all honor and respect. When He had been placed in the tomb, I continued to stand outside weeping and crying. I was overcome with all manner of sorrow, and spoke I then these words: "O, thou Angel Gabriel, thou once said unto to me 'Hail Mary, full of grace.' But behold, now I am full of sorrow! Thou said also to me, 'The Lord is with thee.' But behold, now my Lord and my Son have been removed from me by the grim and inexorable hand of death! And thou likewise didst say unto me, 'Blessed be thou amongst all women'. But behold, now above all other women I am tormented and afflicted with sorrow, and held by all to be most accursed![5] And finally, thou didst declare unto me, 'Blessed be the fruit of thy womb.' But behold, now my Son—that is, the fruit of my womb—is here most wickedly killed, and now lies enclosed in the tomb, His gentle body sorely bruised and full of wounds!"

---

[5] In Luke 1:42, it is actually Elizabeth, rather than Gabriel, who speaks to Mary the words "Blessed art thou among women and blessed is the fruit of thy womb." However, according to ancient tradition, they are understood as being divinely inspired and therefore a continuation of the angel's message. Accordingly, they are regarded as forming part of the Angelic Salutation of Mary.

And when I had concluded these words of despair and anguish, I collapsed down once more upon the earth.

Now, the apostle Saint John, whom Jesus had declared to be my new son while He was upon the cross, was standing by close at hand. And when he saw me thus overcome with grief, he took me up in his arms. For at that time, because of the feebleness of my body and the misery of my heart, I was quite unable to stand. Then John and some faithful women led me from thence back into the city of Jerusalem. While this happened, I was sorely tormented with deep anguish at the thought that I was being separated from the sepulcher where the body of my sweet Son, Jesus, lay lifeless. Indeed, all those who saw me at that time were moved to tears of pity themselves on account of the sorrow and lamentation which they beheld in me.

And then John led me home and took me to my chamber. And he spoke to me these words of comfort and hope, "Now rest thou here, O Mother of my Lord! Place thy hopes in the rising of thy sweet Son, Jesus, Who is my Lord and my God. Cease thou from thy grievous sorrow! And understand well, my Lady, that I am pledged to guard and protect thee as if I were thine own son, although, in truth, I am not worthy even to be thy servant. For I, John, may not be likened to Jesus; I, the son of Zebedee, may not be compared to Him, the Son of God! Nor may I, the servant, be likened to the Lord; nor may the disciple be considered equal to His

Master; nor yet may the creature be likened to the God that created him! But nevertheless I shall guard and honor thee, my reverend Lady, as much as I possibly can, and with all my strength shall I serve thee and attend upon thee!"

With these words, and with others like them, John comforted me greatly in my distress, and he was ready to serve me diligently in accordance with the command of my sweet Son, Jesus. And three days later, when we saw my Son arisen from death to new life, my heart was filled with a radiant happiness which surpassed by far the bitterness and darkness of all my previous sorrows, and which transformed all my tears into heavenly joy!

Blessed be my sweet Son, Jesus! Amen.

THE ROSARY OF THE
SEVEN SORROWS OF MARY

INTRODUCTION

THE ROSARY OF the Seven Sorrows of Mary is a devotion consisting of the Angelic Salutation (the *Hail Mary* or *Ave Maria*) being recited forty-nine times as seven groups of seven. Each of the groups of seven (or septets) is proceeded by an *Our Father* (or *Pater Noster*) and accompanied by meditation on one of the seven sorrows of Our Lady.

The texts given in the following pages are from a small booklet entitled the *Corona dolorosa, seu modus pie meditandi dolores praecipuos B. V. Mariae*[1] and published in 1738. It is designed to guide the reader through this devotion, outlining each of the sorrows for meditation and including a short prayer to Our Lady before each *Hail Mary*.

It is pertinent to note that this form of the Rosary has been granted official approval by the Roman Catholic Church,

---

[1] *The Sorrowful Crown, or a Method of Piously Meditating on the Principal Sorrows of the Blessed Virgin Mary.*

and several popes have decreed particular indulgences to those who pray it.

Pope Benedict XIII, in his Bull *Redemptoris Domini* of September 26, 1724, granted the following:

- an indulgence of two hundred days[2] for each of the Angelic Salutations and Lord's Prayers of this Rosary when said in a church of the Servite Order;

- an indulgence of two hundred days for each of the Angelic Salutations and Lord's Prayers of this Rosary when said in any location, on any Friday, or during Lent, or on any of the feast days of the Blessed Virgin;

- an indulgence of one hundred days for each of the Angelic Salutations and Lord's Prayers of this Rosary when said in any location and on any days others than those specified above; and,

- an indulgence of seven years for anyone who prays the entire Rosary of the Seven Sorrows of Mary.

---

2   *Indulgentiarum doctrina* (1967), the apostolic constitution of Pope Saint Paul VI, reorganized the discipline of indulgences. Norm 4 of the constitution eliminated any determination of days or years and established that all such indulgences would henceforth be designated as "partial" indulgences (see also *CCC* 1471). Indulgences are administered through the Apostolic Penitentiary, and the reader is directed to its *Enchiridion Indulgentiarum: Norma et Concessiones*, or *Handbook on Indulgences*.

Pope Clement XII, in his Bull *Unigeniti Filii* of December 12, 1734, added to the above-listed indulgences the following:

- an indulgence of one hundred years to anyone who receives a set of beads for saying the Rosary of the Seven Sorrows of Mary which has been blessed by a priest of the Servite Order;

- an indulgence of one hundred and fifty years to anyone who recites the Rosary of the Seven Sorrows of Mary on a Monday, Wednesday, or Friday, or any feast day of the Blessed Virgin using a set of beads blessed by a priest of the Servite Order;

- an indulgence of two hundred years for anyone who recites the Rosary of the Seven Sorrows of Mary after having made a thorough examination of their conscience and who prays for the exaltation of Holy Mother Church, the eradication of heresies, and the increase of the Catholic faith;

- a plenary indulgence, once a year, to all who make a custom of praying this Rosary at least four times a week, on whatever days they choose; and,

- a plenary indulgence to all who recite this Rosary every day for an entire month, praying for the exaltation of Holy Mother Church, for peace amongst Christian leaders, and for the eradication of heresies.

The faculty to bless beads for the Rosary of the Seven Sorrows of Mary was originally granted exclusively to priests of the Servite Order, with which the devotion is traditionally associated. In 1884, Pope Leo XIII extended this faculty to all priests (both of other religious orders and diocesan clergy) and extended accordingly the indulgences granted by Clement XII.

SEPTET OF THE FIRST SORROW: THE CIRCUMCISION OF CHRIST AND SIMEON'S PROPHECY

THE FIRST SORROW of the Blessed Virgin Mary was when she presented her most holy Son to undergo the prescribed rite of circumcision. It was at that time that she heard the prediction of Simeon that the divine Infant would become a "sign of contradiction" to many and that a sword of sorrow was also destined to pass through her own heart.[3]

---

[3]   See Luke 2:21–35.

Our Father...

I

O Mother most sorrowful! What bitter pain your heart did feel on account of the blood shed by your infant Son at His circumcision. Teach me, I pray, to circumcise all the inordinate or ungoverned passions of my own soul.

Hail Mary...

II

O Virgin most afflicted—through the love and pain which you felt when you received your infant Son, still bleeding from His circumcision, back into your arms—grant, I beseech you, the grace always to receive Christ with the same tender love and affection in the most holy Sacrament of the Eucharist.

Hail Mary...

III

Mother of sorrows, through the pity and compassion which you felt in your heart when you carried your newly-circumcised Son back to your home, wound my heart with the tender pain of compassion towards all those who suffer.

Hail Mary...

IV

Through that anguish and anxiety of mind which the prophetic words of Simeon caused you as you pondered them and wondered over them, grant to me, O Mother, the ability to contemplate your sorrows deeply and sensitively and to penetrate wisely the mysteries of Sacred Scripture.

Hail Mary...

V

O Virgin, your sorrow was renewed when you washed and dressed your newly-circumcised Son and saw again the wound He had suffered. Renew constantly in my own heart my love for Jesus each time I meditate upon all that He suffered for my salvation.

Hail Mary...

VI

Most loving Mother, each time you heard your beloved baby Jesus crying out, your own heart felt that it would burst! Fill me with similar tears whenever I consider the holy and saving wounds of Christ.

Hail Mary...

VII

Virgin most holy, the wound of your Son's circumcision had barely healed when you heard of the wicked plan of Herod to put Him to death, and you were filled with new anguish and tears because of this. Grant that I may also be filled with tears when I consider how that, through my own sins, I have brought about the necessity of Christ's death and contributed to His sufferings.

Hail Mary...

SEPTET OF THE SECOND SORROW: THE FLIGHT INTO EGYPT

THE SECOND SORROW of the Blessed Virgin Mary was when she, together with Jesus and Joseph, was compelled to flee secretly at night into the distant land of Egypt to escape Herod's wicked attempts to kill the holy Infant.[4]

---

4   See Matthew 2:19–22.

Our Father…

I

Mother filled with most bitter grief, you were forced to flee into Egypt with your beloved Son on account of the pride and ambition of Herod. Grant that, through true humility, I may prepare a quiet, safe, and welcoming place of refuge for you and your Son within my heart.

Hail Mary…

II

Most sorrowful Lady, often during this hard journey you beheld your Son, a tender baby, shivering from cold and exposed to rain and wind. Help me to be patient in accepting and enduring all the difficult circumstances and adverse conditions which I may sometimes encounter in the journey of this mortal life.

Hail Mary…

III

Uniquely blessed Virgin and Mother, during your flight to Egypt, you—together with your Son, Jesus, and your spouse, Saint Joseph—bravely sustained hunger and thirst because of the unavoidable shortages of the basic necessities of life—namely, food and drink. Grant that I, like you, may bear all deprivations, poverty, and insufficiencies with a cheerful and patient soul.

Hail Mary…

IV

Virgin most tender, I know that during your flight to Egypt, you endured much fatigue and exhaustion without the least complaint or resentment. Make me diligent and strong in laboring for your sake and for the glory of your Son and His holy Church, and let me not be overly eager in seeking out rest and recreation from my duties.

Hail Mary…

V

Mother of tears, you wept bitterly when you came to know in spirit the slaughter of the innocents which took place through the cruelty and wickedness of Herod. May I also weep sincerely for the pain and distress I have caused others, especially through my own sins and selfishness.

Hail Mary...

VI

Beloved Mother—through the merits of the long and lonely exile which you underwent during those years in Egypt—teach me to accept the trials and adversities of this life, even if they last for a long time.

Hail Mary...

VII

Mother most patient, when you learned that the angel had revealed to Joseph that the appointed time for leaving Egypt and returning home had arrived, you realized that this meant having to repeat an arduous and perilous journey, with all its discomforts and hardships. Grant to me the grace to accept the will of God and of my legitimate superiors with humility and obedience, even when it involves undergoing hardships and difficulties.

Hail Mary...

SEPTET OF THE THIRD SORROW: WHEN THE BOY JESUS WAS LOST FOR THREE DAYS[5]

THE THIRD SORROW of the most precious Virgin occurred when her Son, Jesus—then a boy of just twelve years of age—was lost in Jerusalem, and she, together with Joseph, sought Him with great anxiety and concern for three days before finally finding Him in the Temple.[6]

---

[5] The prayers in this series also include meditations about Mary's reactions to the sufferings and persecutions of Christ up to His passion, as well as the beginning of the passion itself, until the sentence of death was passed upon Him.

[6] See Luke 2:41–50.

Our Father...

I

O Mother of mercy, when your Son was lost to you, you suffered immense anxiety and sorrow because of your separation from Him. Grant, I pray, that I may never lose sight of Jesus through my sins and negligence but may constantly keep His beloved presence before my eyes and always be close to Him.

Hail Mary...

II

Most sorrowful Lady, as your divine Son grew up and matured, so too did your own sorrows increase, for you sensed that His many rivals and foes were beginning to look upon Him with envy and suspicion and even then beginning to plot against His life. Help me to follow the example of your Son and to remain constant and quietly patient in the face of all opposition and persecution.

Hail Mary...

III

O Mother, afflicted with the bitterness of pain, it was the same human blood that you had conceived in your womb which your Son sweated in the garden of Gethsemane. Grant that I may love your Son just as you loved Him and be ready to express this love, even with my own tears and blood whenever necessary.

Hail Mary…

IV

Suffering Mother, you were filled with unspeakable disappointment and regret when you heard that the treacherous Judas Iscariot had betrayed your beloved Son. Fill me with genuine remorse for all the times I too have betrayed your Son through committing sin, and thus have brought disappointment and sorrow to you also.

Hail Mary…

V

Desolate Mother, when you heard that Jesus had been arrested, you were struck with an inexpressible dread and horror. Grant me the grace of amending and correcting all my sins, vices, failings, and negligence whereby I have hurt your Son or failed to show Him due reverence and love.

Hail Mary…

VI

Virgin Mother, your heart became like a vast sea of sorrow when you witnessed your Son being scourged with whips and crowned with thorns! Indeed, you felt His pain as if it were your own. Make me also to share in the pain which both you and He felt at this time and to experience, through true compassion, the pain of others as if it were my own.

Hail Mary…

VII

O Mother of God, you exceed all other created beings in immaculate purity and perfect sanctity! Through the merits of your grief and suffering when you heard the fateful sentence of death passed against your Son, protect me from the sentence of eternal damnation and never-ending death when I face Him as my Judge on that dreaded final day.

Hail Mary…

SEPTET OF THE FOURTH SORROW: JESUS CARRIES HIS CROSS TO CALVARY

THE FOURTH SORROW of the Blessed Virgin was when she met her most beloved Son as He was carrying the cross upon His shoulders to Calvary, the place of His execution.

Our Father...

I

O Mary, through that maternal love which caused you to follow in the bloodstained footsteps of Jesus, draw me after yourself so that I may share your sorrows and, with you, faithfully follow your Son as He carries the cross of our salvation.

Hail Mary...

II

Virgin most afflicted, your pain and anguish was renewed with each drop of blood which you saw fall to the earth from the body of your beloved Son. Grant me the grace that I myself may not renew or contribute to your sorrows through any lack of restraint of my own vision, or by letting my eyes be directed by idle curiosity, cupidity, or lust.

Hail Mary...

III

O desolate Mother, you beheld your poor Child often to fall under the weight of the cross which He carried as He made His way to Calvary, and then to be goaded on by the cruelty of the executioners. May I never renew or add to the weight which Christ has to bear through my own sins and wickedness.

Hail Mary...

IV

O mournful Mother, how immense was your sorrow when you saw your Son to be stripped of His vestments at the hill of Calvary so that all the wounds which He bore upon His body were once more exposed to your loving eyes! Do not permit me, I beseech you, ever to be stripped of the vestments of grace which I have received through baptism by the diabolical enemies of my soul.

Hail Mary...

V

Through those nails which pierced the hands and feet of Jesus, and, in doing so, pierced your own heart as well, let my heart be pierced with a constant and ardent love for you and for your Son.

Hail Mary...

VI

Mother inconsolable, through that torment with which you witnessed your Son to be affixed to the hard wood of the cross, you yourself almost expired from the very intensity of your grief. May I learn to bear my own crosses with humility and fortitude, especially those which are the result of my own sins.

Hail Mary...

VII

Virgin most sorrowful, you beheld the cross being raised up, and the body of your Son to be tormented terribly as His wounds and pains were renewed by the weight placed upon them. Make me ever mindful, I pray, of the unfathomable magnitude of the suffering which Jesus and you endured for the sake of my sins, and the immense price which he paid for my redemption.

Hail Mary...

SEPTET OF THE FIFTH SORROW: THE DEATH OF JESUS UPON THE CROSS

THE FIFTH SORROW of the Mother of God was when Jesus was raised up on the cross and she witnessed Him die there in pain, all the while being mocked by the malicious crowds.

Our Father…

I

Suffering Mother, you saw and heard your divine and innocent Son being mocked and blasphemed as He hung upon the cross in agony. Grant to me, I pray, that I may help to atone for the derision He then suffered by praising and blessing Him for all eternity in heaven.

Hail Mary…

II

Desolate Mother, through that spirit and love and obedience which transfixed your heart and caused you to accept the apostle Saint John as your adopted son and guardian,[7] help me to be a faithful servant to you, and lovingly accept me as your adopted son or daughter.

Hail Mary…

III

Mother of peerless strength and courage, how immense was the anguish with which you heard your Son cry out in despair to His heavenly Father, "Why hast thou abandoned me?" May I learn to confide and trust in you utterly at all times, even when I have fallen into sin, and most especially at the hour of my death.

Hail Mary…

---

[7] See John 19:26–27.

IV

Lady of sorrows, you endured hearing your Son cry out that He thirsted, yet grieved that you had no means to assuage that thirst. Grant that I may satisfy the thirst of your Son, for He thirsts most of all for my salvation. Help me also to be generous in satisfying the legitimate hungers and needs of my neighbors.

Hail Mary...

V

Most merciful Mother, when your Son died, you witnessed the heavens become dark and the very stones to be torn apart. Grant that the stony hardness of my heart may be softened by vehement contemplation of your sorrows and by true compunction for my sins, especially when my own senses are darkened by the approach of death.

Hail Mary...

VI

Holy Mary, you stood faithfully at the foot of the cross while you underwent the incomprehensible anguish of seeing your only-begotten Son breathing His last. Stand by me too, my Mother, as I struggle to bear the weight of my own many weaknesses and failings.

Hail Mary...

VII

Most merciful Lady, through that pang of sorrow and love which you felt when you saw the side of your beloved Son being torn open by that cruel lance, hide me in the holy wound of that same love from the righteous fury which my sins have merited on the final Day of Judgment.

Hail Mary...

SEPTET OF THE SIXTH SORROW: THE LIFELESS BODY OF CHRIST IS PLACED IN THE ARMS OF HIS MOTHER

THE SIXTH SORROW of Our Lady was when Christ was taken down from the cross, and she received His lifeless and cruelly wounded body into her maternal embrace.

Our Father...

I

Ever-Virgin Mother, when you received the dead and blood-smeared body of your Son into your arms, you embraced Him with indescribable tenderness, kissing His wounds with infinite love and mercy. Teach me to contemplate His saving wounds often and intently with something of the same love and compassion.

Hail Mary...

II

Most patient Lady, the tears you shed as you held the body of Jesus flowed over His tender skin in abundant streams, washing His wounds clean from the copious blood which covered them. May I also wash away the stains of my own sins with tears of true repentance.

Hail Mary...

III

Sweetest Mother, through the triple sorrow which you experienced when you beheld the three nails by which your Son had been affixed to the cross, affix my memory, intellect, and will firmly to constant love of Jesus and you.

Hail Mary...

IV

O Queen of martyrs, how great was your sorrow when you accepted into your hands that bloody crown of thorns, the cause of which was my own proud and impure thoughts! Grant me the grace, I pray, of always resisting such wicked thoughts so that by doing so I may help to alleviate your grief.

Hail Mary...

V

Afflicted Mother, when you looked upon the wounds of your Son, they were indelibly imprinted upon your memory for all eternity. Grant that I may likewise always remember how much you and your Son suffered for the sake of my redemption!

Hail Mary...

VI

Most faithful Woman, as you held the body of your beloved Son in your arms, you offered Him up to His heavenly Father in atonement for the sins of the world. I pray that the glorious fruit of His passion—that is, our eternal salvation—may never be lost to me or negated through my sins.

Hail Mary…

VII

O Mary, before your Son was taken from your arms to be buried in the tomb, you tenderly affixed one last and infinitely loving kiss upon Him. Grant that I may never be separated from your Son, especially during the hour of my death. Although at that time my soul and body shall be separated from each other, may they never be separated from the love of Jesus and of you!

Hail Mary…

SEPTET OF THE SEVENTH AND FINAL SORROW: CHRIST IS PLACED IN HIS TOMB

THE SEVENTH SORROW of Mary, the gracious refuge of and advocate for all sinners, was when she witnessed the body of Jesus enclosed within the silent darkness of the tomb.

Our Father...

I

Most courageous and strong Woman, with sweeping waves of bitter grief, you were forcibly separated from the body of your beloved Son, and you saw this same dear body being enclosed in the darkness of the tomb. May my own heart remain likewise firmly closed to all the wicked temptations and deceitful vanities of this passing world.

Hail Mary...

II

Tearful Virgin, when your Son was placed in the tomb, you longed to be buried there with Him! Grant, I pray, that I may be buried with Christ in spirit and find my true life, not in the external world, but hidden within Him.

Hail Mary...

III

Grieving Mother, you wept for the stubborn and cruel hardness of the hearts of the people, which you found reflected in the hardness of the stone from which your Son's tomb was fashioned. Soften the stoniness of my heart by your holy tears, that it may more readily receive the sacred body of Jesus.

Hail Mary...

IV

Sorrowful Maiden, amongst all your afflictions and tribulations you were left with Saint John as your unique source of consolation and protection. Grant that, in my devotion to you, I may serve and love you as your adopted son or daughter, just like the holy Saint John.

Hail Mary...

V

Gentle Virgin, when you at last departed from the tomb of Christ, you bore with you the bitter memory of every detail of your Son's passion and death. Help me to carry in my heart the loving memory of your Son's wounds at all times, and most especially during times of trial, temptation, and tribulation.

Hail Mary...

VI

Mary, you were bereaved of your only-begotten Son, Whom you had witnessed undergoing much labor and suffering, both in His life and death, in order to turn the people from their sins. And yet many of them remained obstinate and stubborn, refusing to hear His words or to receive His grace. May I never add to your sorrows by my own obstinance in sin or error, nor by my pride and stubbornness.

Hail Mary...

VII

Mother most loving, through the Holy Spirit, you perceived in advance all that was to come until the end of time. Thus you saw clearly that many thousands of Christian souls, for whom your Son had shed His blood, would lose the fruit of His passion—which is eternal salvation—through sin, infidelity, and heresy. And this was to you a source of untold grief. May I never be amongst those who lose this glorious fruit of eternal life, but may I labor strenuously and constantly for my own salvation and for that of my neighbor.

Hail Mary...

CLOSING PRAYERS

FOLLOWING THESE SEVEN septets, the Hail Mary is said three more times in memory of the tears shed by the Blessed Virgin.

I

O Mother most glorious and yet humble, through all the tears which you shed during the life of your divine Son, gain for us a spirit of profound humility against the evil spirit of pride.

Hail Mary…

II

O Mother most chaste and inviolate, through all the tears which you shed during the passion and death of your only-begotten Son, gain for us a spirit of purity against the unclean spirit of lust.

Hail Mary...

III

O radiant Queen of Heaven, through the tears of joy which you shed after the resurrection of your beloved Son, gain for us a spirit of unshakable faith and devotion against the inconstant and deceptive spirit of the world.[8]

Hail Mary...

The Rosary of the Seven Sorrows of Mary is concluded with a recitation either of the Creed or of the Stabat Mater.

---

[8]   In the original Latin text, this final prayer intention is specifically directed to vocations to the Servite Order. The present translator has modified it slightly to be suitable for general use.